HERB GARDENING

■ Step by Step to Growing Success ■

Jessica Houdret

CROWOOD GARDENING GUIDES

...orough
...SN8 2HR

© The Crowood Press Ltd 1991

This impression 1992

British Library Cataloguing in Publication Data

Houdret, Jessica
   Herb gardening.
   1. Gardens. Herbs. Cultivation
   I. Title
   635.7

ISBN 1 85223 410 5

Acknowledgements
Grateful thanks to all those who welcomed me to their gardens and herb nurseries to take photographs, and to those who supplied me with plans and planting lists and gave up valuable time to give me help and advice. My special thanks to Simon and Judith Hopkinson of Hollington Nurseries (who made this project possible in the first place), to Richard Scott of The Herb Farm (who designed the 'thyme river') and also to the Marchioness of Salisbury, Mr Paul Stearn, Dr Jane Renfrew, Mr David Lee, Mrs Vivienne Trusler, Mrs Sybil Spencer, Mrs Grant and Mrs Rosemary Verey.

Picture credits
All photographs by the author.
All colour artwork by Claire Upsdale-Jones.

Typeset by Acorn Bookwork, Salisbury, Wiltshire
Printed and bound by Times Publishing Group, Singapore

Contents

Introduction

WHY GROW HERBS?

Herbs are rewarding plants to grow, being both decorative and useful. They also smell good, releasing their aromatic fragrance as you brush against them or pick the leaves. When it comes to planning how to plant them, they are versatile, lending themselves equally to both formal and informal schemes, and are quick to establish, so that a mature effect can soon be achieved.

The benefits of growing herbs are many. The problem can be knowing where to start, which plants to choose, and how best to plant them. This book aims to take you through the stages of familiarizing yourself with the plants, of learning how to propagate and cultivate them, and of deciding on the most suitable design for your garden that will best fulfil your particular needs.

WHAT IS A HERB?

Herbs are plants with properties which can be of benefit to man. Traditionally this has included plants with culinary, aromatic or medicinal qualities. Through the ages, the term 'herb' has encompassed different groups of plants. In the sixteenth century, plants that we now call vegetables, such as carrots and onions, were known as 'pot herbs' and 'salad herbs' included lettuces and radishes. Therefore, when deciding on authentic plants for a herb garden, the choice is wide and boundaries vague. Mrs Grieve in a A

Fig 1   A long, narrow border, planted to take account of the varying heights of herbs.

Modern Herbal, a definitive work published in the 1930s, lists more than a thousand plants as herbs.

In the following pages, just over fifty traditional herbs are described, along with some of the varieties (or species) available in addition to

Fig 2   Lovage, shown here with fennel in the foreground, can grow to well over 6ft (1.8m).

the common or best-known member of each genus. This selection should provide a good choice for a variety of different herb gardens.

GETTING TO KNOW THE PLANTS

First get to know the plants. The best way to do this is to visit as many herb gardens as possible, so that you can see the plants when they are mature. Remember that a neat little lovage plant in a 3in (7.5cm) pot in the garden centre gives little indication that it will reach 6ft (1.8m) and spread sideways too. As well as noting heights, find out as much as you can about habits of growth, such as whether they are lax and untidy or neat and compact.

Notice the colours and textures of the leaves. You will find every shade of green, as well as golden, silver, bronze and purple and a whole range of variegations. Foliage can also be anything from feathery and delicate to thick and glossy.

Discover the colours of the flowers and time of flowering. Although herbs are often grown primarily for their leaves, many do have colourful and showy flowers as can be seen by a bank of mist blue catmint or a mass of gaudy gold pot marigolds.

Look out for specialist herb nurseries with display gardens (see the list on pages 124–6) where the plants are usually well labelled. These gardens have the advantage of being designed with the needs of the customer in mind and are often planned as separate, self-contained sections, any of which could stand on their own. Also, with any luck, there should be someone knowledgeable on hand to advise, or help with identification.

There are botanic gardens and herb gardens open to the public at National Trust houses and stately homes. Not all such gardens are on the grand scale and even those which are can provide valuable inspiration for more modest projects. You can learn a lot from other people's planting schemes, and borrow ideas that appeal to you, a border of chives around roses, for example, or a bank of silvery wormwood, surrounded by the dark green oak-like leaves of wall germander. It helps to keep a notebook to jot down what you see, and photographs can be

Fig 3   Pot marigolds make a vivid splash of colour in a 'herb wheel'.

Fig 4   Chives are sympathetic bed companions for graceful old-fashioned
roses – this one is 'Constance Spry'.

useful as an *aide-mémoire* when it comes to making your own plans.

The Plant Profiles in Chapter 1 should help you with other important facts about the plants, such as whether they are annuals, biennials or perennials, whether they die down in winter or remain evergreen, and whether they should be grown from cuttings or seeds. Information is also given for individual plant preferences, as regards type of soil, sun or shade, damp or dry conditions.

The good news is that herbs are, on the whole, easy-going plants which are not difficult to grow. This is, perhaps, one of their main attractions.

DECIDING ON A DESIGN

At the same time that you are learning about the plants, take note of overall designs that appeal to you and that you may be able to copy or adapt to your own purposes. Once again, take photographs, make notes or draw simple reference maps to remind you of the layout and special features in other people's gardens. A herb garden can be anything from an elaborate box-edged parterre to a small area set aside in the border or flower-bed. Whether you want to grow a few herbs for the kitchen, or if you have something more ambitious in mind, time spent planning will be well rewarded.

7

CHAPTER 1

Plant Profiles

This chapter outlines the characteristics of each herb, giving a short description, its status of annual, perennial or biennial, its height when mature, any specific growing requirements and its most common uses. Suggestions are given as to which herbs it is best to buy initially to get your garden started and which ones you would do better to grow from seed. Methods of propagation, in order to increase your stocks, are also covered.

For ease of reference the herbs are listed in alphabetical order under their common name with the Latin name in italics. They are arranged under two main headings: Culinary Herbs and Ornamental and Fragrant Herbs. This is not to say that the categories are mutually exclusive. All the culinary herbs could find a place in a general herb garden or in one designed primarily as an ornamental feature, and some of the herbs listed in the ornamental section, such as rose, hyssop and pineapple sage, can be used in cooking.

Herbs are by definition 'useful' plants and the ornamental herbs included, as well as being used to provide fragrance in the home, can all be put to practical purpose to make beauty preparations or home remedies and herb teas. Where appropriate, these uses are briefly indicated. Many of them also have a long tradition as medicinal herbs but, apart from the home remedies referred to, the medicinal uses of herbs are beyond the scope of this book.

There is a final section which lists Invasive Herbs. These are ones that are best avoided, unless you have a specific reason to grow them, have plenty of room, or are prepared to exercise ruthless control.

It is important to know the growing span of your herbs. As with other garden plants, they can be divided into three main categories:

1. Annuals. These grow, flower and die in the course of one year.
2. Biennials. These start into growth one year and flower and die the following year.
3. Perennials. These last for several years. This category includes:
(a) Evergreens and shrubby perennials. Most of these keep their foliage throughout the winter, although some, like lemon verbena, are deciduous.
(b) Herbaceous perennials. Their top growth dies off each autumn, and it should be cut back to the roots, leaving room for fresh growth to come through in the spring.

CULINARY HERBS

The Top Twenty

A comprehensive selection of twenty herbs, which will fulfil the needs of all but the most ambitious cook:

Angelica	Basil
Bay	Borage
Chervil	Chives
Coriander	Dill
Fennel	Lovage
Marjoram	Mint
Parsley	Rosemary
Sage	Savory, Summer
Savory, Winter	Sweet Cicely
Tarragon	Thyme

Twelve to Start

For those who would like to start with fewer plants, the following selection could be made:

Basil	Bay
Chervil	Chives
Marjoram/Oregano	Mint
Parsley	Rosemary
Sage	Savory, Winter
Tarragon	Thyme

Eight for Containers

A small container garden could be based on just eight different herbs, grown in pots and tubs on the patio:

Basil	Bay
Chives	Mint
Parsley	Rosemary
Savory	Thyme

A Few Extras

If you have room and would like to include some more unusual herbs, try:

Salad Burnet	Sorrel
Welsh Onion	

Herbs with Edible Flowers

Flowers add a decorative touch to salads and sweet dishes. Any of the following are safe to eat:

Borage	Hyssop
Nasturtium	Pinks
Rose	Pot Marigold

Angelica *Angelica archangelica*

Description Botanically, angelica is a biennial but it often does not flower until its third year. It is a tall plant which grows to 6–8ft (1.8–2.5m)

Fig 5 *Angelica is a useful culinary herb and makes an architectural feature in the border. It has spectacular globe-shaped flower-heads.*

and makes an impressive architectural feature in the border with large glossy leaves growing on fragrant hollow stems. The flowers (which usually appear in late June or July) consist of small greenish-yellow florets which form spectacular, globe-shaped umbels.

Propagation Start off by buying a plant. One would be sufficient for most purposes. Angelica usually self-seeds freely, so, once you have an

9

established plant, you are unlikely to need to propagate others. If the seedlings come up in the wrong place, they can be rooted out, saving the strongest to transplant to the site of your choice. If you do want to grow your own plants from scratch, propagation is by seed. Angelica seeds soon lose their potency, so, for best results, do not buy seed but collect some from your first plant, allow to ripen and sow in August or September. The seeds will overwinter and come up the following spring.

Cultivation   Angelica tolerates most conditions but is happiest in a semi-shaded position with fairly rich, damp soil. It is too big to grow successfully in a pot.

Uses   The young stems can be candied, or cooked with rhubarb and other tart fruit to reduce the acidity.

Basil *Ocimum basilicum (also known as sweet basil)*

Description   Basil is a tender annual. The leaves are ovate and soft, almost fleshy, with an unmistakable warm spicy aroma. The flowers are white and appear on spikes at the stem ends from midsummer onwards. As for most culinary herbs, the flowers should be cut off before they can form, to maintain leaf quality and, for annuals such as basil, to prolong the plant's life.

Varieties   Purple basil can also be used in cooking but, with its striking purple-red leaves and pink flower spikes, its chief virtue is in its decorative value.

Propagation   Two or three plants should be enough to supply the average kitchen over the season, so you would be justified in buying plants each year to save trouble. If you do want to raise your own plants, do not be deterred by basil's reputation for being difficult. Follow the guidelines set out in Chapter 2, under Propagating Techniques, for success every time.

Cultivation   Basil likes damp soil and plenty of sun. For fool-proof maintenance, grow on in a large pot rather than planting out in the garden, where it will be at the mercy of slugs and snails. Use a peat-based compost in the pot, keep well-watered and stand in a sunny and sheltered position. For nice bushy plants, snip off the top shoots, and cut off flower-heads as soon as you notice them forming.

Uses   A first-choice culinary herb, much used in Mediterranean cookery, basil's affinity with tomatoes is well known, and is the classic flavour for *ratatouille* and pasta dishes. It must be used fresh as it develops a different and infinitely inferior taste when dried.

Bay *Laurus nobilis*

Description   Bay is an evergreen tree or shrub. In Britain, under favourable conditions, it will grow to about 30ft (9m) and in warmer climates even taller. The oval leaves are dark green, tough and glossy. Clusters of inconspicuous greenish-yellow flowers appear at the base of the leaves in early summer.

Propagation   This is done from cuttings, although it is not the easiest of herbs to propagate, unless you have a heated greenhouse, as the cuttings need warmth and protection through the winter. They are also very slow growing. If you do want to have a go, take 4in (10cm) heel cuttings in August or September.

Cultivation   Once established, the bay tree can be treated as hardy, in the south of England at least, but make sure you choose a sheltered, sunny site. It is wise to give a young bay some protection during its first winter after being planted out, as hard frost is likely to turn the leaves brown, although they should recover in the spring.

Bays lend themselves to being raised as standards or cut into pyramid shapes and grown in containers. Use loam-based compost and do not

Fig 6 A mop-head bay tree, surrounded by lavender, is the centre-piece in this culinary herb garden. Basil is best grown in pots. Purple basil is on the right and sweet basil to the left.

overwater. If grown in pots, bay should be sheltered in the winter in a frost-free greenhouse.

Uses The leaves are good, fresh or dry. Add to soups, stews, casseroles, marinades, or use as a garnish for pâtés and for sweet dishes such as citrus sorbets served in scooped out orange skins. A bay leaf is an essential component of a bouquet garni.

Borage *Borago officinalis*

Description Borage is a hardy annual which grows to about 3ft 6in (1m). The stems and leaves are grey-green, coarse and hairy. Its appeal is in the dainty star-shaped flowers which are a glorious blue, with occasional pink ones,

and grow in drooping clusters, attracting bees. Borage looks best planted in drifts of three or more. One plant on its own does not do itself justice.

Propagation As with most annual herbs, especially when several plants are needed, it really is a waste of money to buy borage ready-grown, and if you try to transplant one that is coming into flower, and therefore three-quarters through its life cycle, it is a waste of time as well. You will probably only need to sow seeds once because borage self-seeds freely. Sow straight into the ground in April, or in seed trays under cover in March, with a view to transplanting to a final position once the ground has warmed up. Alternatively, plant seeds in autumn to overwinter and flower in spring.

Fig 7   Star-shaped borage flowers can be used to garnish a salad or to float in summer drinks.

Cultivation   Borage needs little cultivation. If the plants spring up where you do not want them, pull them out, or transplant them to where you do, leaving plenty of room between them, at least 1ft (30cm). Borage does well in stony or free-draining soil; give it a sunny position as well and it will thrive. Once it has finished flowering, it will sprawl untidily and so it is advisable to pull it out. Borage is not suitable as a container plant.

Uses   The flowers can be floated in drinks, or used to garnish salads and desserts. They can be dried or candied. The leaves have a faint cucumber flavour and make a refreshing addition to a fruit or wine cup. They are also rich in mineral salts and can, therefore, be incorporated into cooked dishes for those who want to cut their salt intake.

Chervil *Anthriscus cerefolium*

Description   Chervil is a hardy annual. It has a delicate flavour and light green lacy foliage. It grows in low clumps about 1ft (30cm) high.

Propagation   Buying one or two chervil plants is a waste of time and money. It does not transplant well and is likely to run to seed quickly, especially in hot, dry weather. Buy a packet of seed instead and grow your own. With a reasonably mild winter, it is possible to have a year-round supply, grown outdoors, of this subtly flavoured plant. As it is ready for cutting six to eight weeks after putting in the seeds, this can be achieved by successional sowing. Starting in January or February (if the ground is workable) sow at six-week intervals through to the end of May or early June. For an autumn and winter supply, sow again in August and October, or simply allow the summer crops to seed themselves. Seeds should be scattered where they are to grow, and lightly covered with soil.

Cultivation   If you cut it right back, once it is ready for use, chervil will sprout again from the base. However, if you do that it will not self-seed as well. This is one of the few herbs that does not mind a cool, wet climate with little sun. For container-growing, sow the seeds in a large pot, thinning out if necessary and harvesting once the leaves are well developed.

Uses   Its delicate, sweetish flavour enhances egg and fish dishes. In the classic combination, *fines herbes*, it brings out the flavour of the other herbs, which are tarragon, parsley and chives.

Chives *Allium schoenoprasum*

Description   Chives are perennial and the smallest member of the onion family, with clumps of spiky leaves 6–8in (15–20cm) high. Chives make pretty border plants, as the mauve flower globes, which appear in May and June, are very decorative. However, if you want a good supply of leaves for cooking, be sure to snip off the flower-heads before they form.

Propagation   It is easiest to start with two or three plants and, after a season or two, lift them in spring or autumn and split up the close-growing clumps of little bulbs to make new plants. Chives can also be grown from seed but it takes some time to achieve thick clumps suitable for cutting.

Cultivation Chives should be divided every two or three years, if they are to remain lush and vigorous. They will grow in most garden soils, but keep them well watered. They grow well in pots.

Uses Snip them into salads, soft cheeses and dips and over new potatoes. They are a component of *fines herbes.*

Coriander *Coriandrum sativum*

Description Coriander is a strong-smelling, spicy herb which grows to about 2ft (60cm) and is a hardy annual. The lower, parsley-like leaves, which develop first, are the ones to eat, the upper ones, which develop with the flowers, are much finer and more feathery. The flowers carried in umbels, are white tinged with mauve. The seeds are quite large and round.

Propagation It is best to grow coriander from seed rather than buying plants. Like chervil, coriander does not much like being transplanted and will run to seed more quickly if this is done. Sow the seeds in their final position in spring or, for an early crop the following year, in autumn.

Cultivation If you want to grow coriander chiefly for seeds it will do well in a fairly light soil and full sun. But if leaves are the priority, then you should, firstly, take the seed source into account: some American varieties of coriander, which they call 'Cilantro', produce leafier plants. Also, premature flowering is brought about by stress from being kept short of water in poor, dry soil, and by long exposure to light. The best coriander-growing areas of the world are near the equator where daylight is always twelve hours. In temperate climates, avoid sowing too early in the year, as the long daylight hours will

Fig 8   Coriander. The lower leaves are the ones to eat. The upper, feathery leaves appear with the flowers.

encourage the plant to rush into flower. Coriander is not very suitable for container growing.

Uses Both the relatively mild, sweetish seeds and the pungent leaves are used in cookery. The leaves are added to curries and spicy dishes, the seeds complement both sweet and savoury food.

Dill *Anethum graveolens*

Description Dill is a hardy annual. It looks very like fennel but does not grow so tall, reaching only 2ft–2ft 6in (60–75cm). It has feathery leaves and yellow flowers borne in flat umbels.

Propagation Grow it from seed. Although it can be started off in seed trays, dill is not the easiest herb to transplant successfully. It is best to sow the seeds in April, straight into the ground. For a steady supply of fresh leaves, make successional sowings.

Cultivation A well-drained soil and plenty of sun is best for dill. It can be grown in pots on the patio, although it tends to look a bit straggly. Several plants massed together in a large tub is the solution to this.

Uses The leaves (sometimes called dillweed) are good in fish dishes. The seeds are used in pickles and in Scandinavian cookery.

Fennel *Foeniculum vulgare* (also known as green fennel)

Description Fennel is a short-lived perennial; in other words, the plant deteriorates, and sometimes dies, after two or three years. Fennel grows to 5–6ft (1.5–1.8m) and has thick stems and bright green, feathery leaves. The yellow flowers bloom from July to September, making it a decorative border plant as well as a culinary herb. As it is grown for its seeds as much as for the leaf, there is no need to follow the general culinary herb rule of cutting off blooms.

Fig 9 Fennel's feathery foliage and yellow flower clusters make it a decorative border plant, as well as a good culinary herb with an aniseed flavour.

Varieties Bronze fennel, which, as its name implies, has decorative purplish-bronze leaves, can be grown as a culinary herb but is really more suitable as an ornamental. (The bulbous rooted fennel, sold as a vegetable, is Florence fennel, also called sweet fennel, *Foeniculum dulce*. It looks much the same as green fennel when growing, although it is generally a little smaller. It is an annual.)

Propagation For green and bronze fennel: if you only have space for one or two of these plants, you may prefer to start by buying them. If you want to propagate your own, grow from seed. Start the seeds off in a seed tray in March or April (no exceptional heat is needed) and plant out the seedlings when they are sturdy, but not too big and well-established. Green fennel usually self-seeds prolifically.

Cultivation Fennel is a good-natured plant and thrives in most soils and in dry, sunny conditions. Cut it back after flowering and it will sprout again from the base to produce a second crop of leaf. It dies down in winter to emerge again in early spring. Fennel is not suitable for container growing.

Uses Use the leaves, which have a stronger more aniseed flavour than dill, in fish dishes. The seeds are delicious added to stir-fry dishes or mixed into bread or biscuits.

Hyssop *Hyssopus officinalis*

(See the section on Ornamental Herbs for more information.)

Uses The leaves were at one time a popular culinary herb, but they are rather strong-tasting and undistinguished and its chief use in the kitchen today is as an edible flower. The flower spikes are an intense blue (there are also pink and white ones, but blue is the most usual) and make interesting decorations for salads and sweet dishes.

Fig 10 Deep-blue hyssop flowers give a salad an unusual, aromatic flavour.

Lovage *Levisticum officinale*

Description Lovage is a tall, dense, herbaceous perennial with thick stems and glossy, dark green celery-like leaves. It eventually grows to about 6ft (1.8m), spreading sideways to become a sizeable plant. The greenish-yellow flowers, which are not very decorative, are borne on flat umbels at the top of the stems.

Propagation One plant is sufficient for most small gardens and so it is best to buy one. However, it is not difficult to grow from seed, although germination can be slow.

Cultivation Lovage is an undemanding plant but, in order to flourish and supply plenty of green leaf, it needs to be kept watered and grown in reasonably rich soil to which compost has been added. Keep cutting it back to encourage plenty of leafy growth. If you do let it flower, cut it down to the roots afterwards and it will sprout again to provide a second crop. Cut it back to base once again when it dies back in the autumn. Lovage is too large and deep-rooted to be suitable as a pot-grown subject.

Uses Lovage tends to be underrated as a culinary herb, despite its interesting, strong and spicy flavour. Add the leaves to soups, stews and sauces, and snip sparingly over salads, baked potatoes and other cooked vegetables.

Marjoram/Oregano *Origanum* species

Description and Varieties There is often confusion over marjoram and oregano. The Latin name for all the marjorams is *Origanum*, and the herb known as 'oregano' is wild marjoram or *Origanum vulgare*.

The marjorams to grow for culinary use are:

Sweet Marjoram *Origanum majorana* a half-hardy annual with pale, grey-green leaves and white, or occasionally palest pink, flowers, which grow in little knotted clusters around the stem – this being the inspiration for its other common name 'knotted marjoram'. It grows to 8–10in (20–25cm) high and has the most refined flavour of the marjorams.

Pot Marjoram *Origanum onites* a hardy perennial, with darker leaves, pinky-mauve flowers and a stronger taste. It has a less upright, more spreading, habit of growth than the annual marjoram, with the foliage growing to about 8in (20cm) and the flower stems reaching 2ft (60cm).

Wild Marjoram *Origanum vulgare* (Commonly known as oregano) is the strongest-tasting of the marjoram group, and possesses an even more pungent flavour when grown in its native Mediterranean climate and soil. Its bushy growth is sustained on a creeping root-stock. The stems and slightly hairy leaves are often tinged with red and the flowers are a deep rose-purple. It grows to about 2ft (60cm). There are also some attractive decorative marjorams, which are listed under Ornamental and Fragrant Herbs.

Propagation Grow the annual sweet marjoram from seed. The others must be propagated from cuttings or by dividing the clumps in early spring or autumn. Start off by buying named plants from a knowledgeable herb nursery.

Cultivation The marjorams come from the Mediterranean and, for the most part, prefer a light, dry soil and sunny situation. They are inclined to sprawl once they have flowered. Cut them back well to keep them neat and to maintain a good supply of leaves. Marjorams can be grown successfully in pots.

Uses The warm, aromatic flavour of marjoram makes it suitable for meat dishes and stuffings.

Mint *Mentha* species

Varieties There are many kinds of mint. For culinary purposes, the best ones are spearmint, *Mentha spicata*, and Bowles mint, *Mentha rotundifolia*, (Bowles variety), which is a hybrid of applemint, *Mentha rotundifolia*, and spearmint, *Mentha spicata*.

Peppermint, *Mentha piperita*, is the one to grow for peppermint tea. Recognize it by the distinctive purplish-bronze stems and shiny, dark green leaves, also tinged with purple.

Description The mints are herbaceous perennials which grow on creeping root-stocks. Spearmint has bright green, sharply pointed leaves of a rough, wrinkled texture. It grows to about 2ft (60cm). Bowles mint has soft, woolly leaves which are rounder and a greyer shade of green than those of spearmint. It is also a slightly taller plant, reaching about 3ft (90cm). All mints grow on shallow-rooting, creeping underground stems.

Propagation Start by buying plants or begging a root from a friend. Mints should be propagated from cuttings, which root very readily. Take root cuttings in early spring by lifting the underground stems and cutting them into pieces, making sure each piece has a joint. Put the pieces of root in a seed tray in damp compost, covering lightly with more compost. Alternatively, take cuttings from young shoots.

Do not attempt to propagate mint from seed, even though there are packets on offer, as it will not come true to type.

Cultivation This is one of the plants of which people are frightened, believing it will take over. However, in a dry, free-draining soil, mint is not particularly invasive. In a damp, richer soil, if it does grow too prolifically, restrict the roots by growing the plants in a bucket, or kitchen bowl (with the bottom cut out to ensure good drainage) sunk into the ground. As mint is shallow-rooting, it can also be prevented from spreading

Fig 11   Grow mint with its roots confined in a bucket to prevent it spreading in a small herb garden.

with brick or tile divisions surrounding it. It grows best in a damp soil with plenty of added compost. Keep cutting it back and dry any surplus for winter use in the kitchen or to add to a fragrant pot-pourri.

It is also a good idea to dig it all out and replant every three or four years as it has a tendency to develop rust disease if left in one place too long. If you are unlucky enough to buy a plant with this disease, you will not cure it. The only thing to do is to dig it up, destroy it and start again.

Mint can be grown satisfactorily in containers, provided you choose one large enough not to restrict the roots or it will strangle itself. In any case, you will need to start it afresh each year, which involves taking it out of the pot and dividing the roots.

Uses   A good and plentiful supply of fresh mint is a must for any cook. It is used to make mint sauce and mint jelly, to give a fresh tang to summer salads, to snip over new potatoes, peas and other vegetables, to stir into dips and soft cheeses, chutneys and relishes, to put into sweet dishes, especially fruit salads and ice-cream, to add to wine or fruit cups and as a garnish for a wide variety of dishes.

Nasturtium *Tropaeolum majus*

(See the section on Ornamental Herbs for more information.)

Uses   Both the leaves and flowers of this familiar garden annual can be used in salads. The leaves, which are high in Vitamin C, have a strong, peppery taste. The seeds can be pickled and used instead of capers.

Parsley *Petroselinum crispum*

Description   Parsley is a biennial. This is the familiar, curly-leaved parsley, which is usually 8in–1ft (20–30cm) tall.

Varieties   The flat, or fern-leaved, parsleys, popular on the continent, are also well worth growing and are considered by some to have a superior flavour. They grow a little taller than curly parsley and are hardier through the winter.

Propagation   Parsley is another plant that some people find difficult to propagate. For advice on growing parsley successfully from seed, see the section in Chapter 2, page 56.

Cultivation   Parsley likes a damp, rich soil and plenty of sun. In dry weather, keep it well watered and mulched with compost. Being a biennial, it flowers in its second year. To prolong its life, cut it back hard before it has a chance to flower, but if you let some run to seed, provided the conditions are favourable, it will self-seed, ensuring the next year's supply. Although all parsley is reasonably hardy, the flat-leaved varieties stand up better to greater cold. They also tolerate a dry soil better. Parsley is highly suitable to grow in pots or containers, where it is possible to be sure of fulfilling its requirements.

Uses   Of all the herbs, parsley is still the number one best-seller. It has many uses in cooking and is ubiquitous as a garnish but, as it contains valuable vitamins (including A, B and C) and minerals, it seems a pity to leave it on the side of the plate.

Pot Marigold *Calendula officinalis*

(*See* the section on Ornamental Herbs for more information.)

Uses   It is important to use only the old English Pot Marigold, or *Calendula*, for culinary purposes. Under no circumstances substitute French or African marigolds (*Tagetes*), as these are poisonous. The petals, which dry well, can be scattered on salads and sweet dishes, or added to herb cheeses, risottos and paellas. Although sometimes recommended as the 'poor man's saffron', pot marigold is chiefly for colour and is not able to match the flavour of the real thing, which comes from the saffron crocus.

Rose

(*See* section on Ornamental Herbs for more information.)

Description and Cultivation   Rose was once used to make a wide range of preserves, comfits and candies. Any fragrant, preferably pink or red rose, is suitable for culinary use. Ensure that the flowers have not been sprayed with chemicals. Spray, if necessary, early in the season before buds form, and grow chives and garlic nearby to deter pests.

Uses   Snip off the white heel, which can be bitter, at the base of each petal before use. Use petals in syllabubs and sorbets, ice-cream and cheesecakes, adding distilled rosewater for extra flavour. Scatter fresh petals on fruit salads, or crystallize them with sugar and egg-white for later use.

Rosemary *Rosmarinus officinalis*

Description   Rosemary is an evergreen shrub from the Mediterranean coast, with spiky, highly aromatic leaves and dainty, pale blue flowers in spring.

Varieties   There is a prostrate kind and several unusual species with varying flower colours, but beware, some of these are not at all hardy.

Propagation   Although it can be grown from seed, taking cuttings is the best method and they strike quite easily. Take the cuttings in early summer after flowering.

Cultivation   Rosemary prefers a well-drained soil and plenty of sun. It is not always completely hardy, although it can be treated as such in the temperate climates, so give it a sheltered south-facing position in the protection of a wall or hedges, if possible. It can be grown in pots or tubs. Trim to promote bushy growth and make sure that you give a pot-grown rosemary winter protection.

Uses   Rosemary has an affinity with lamb and adds interest to a marinade. It has a very strong flavour and should be used with discretion in cookery.

Sage *Salvia officinalis*

Description   The common or garden grey-leaved sage is the best kind to grow for culinary use. An evergreen, shrubby perennial, it has showy violet-blue flowers in late spring or early summer. There are narrow-leaved and broad-leaved forms of common sage.

Varieties   There are many attractive ornamental sages. The dramatic-looking purple sage can also be used in cooking, but golden sage and tricolour sage are ornamental plants.

Propagation   Garden sage can be grown from seed but named and ornamental varieties must be grown from cuttings, or layered. If you grow sage in a pot, pinch out the tips to keep it compact.

Fig 12   Ordinary garden sage can be grown from seed. It has violet-blue flowers in early summer.

Cultivation   Sage grows wild in the Mediterranean region and it is another herb that flourishes in light, dry soil and full sun. It can get straggly and untidy, so keep it well trimmed and renew the plants every four to six years.

Uses   A very strong-flavoured herb which complements strong-tasting meat like game, or meat and poultry with a high fat content, such as pork, goose or duck. It is traditionally used in stuffings.

Salad Burnet *Sanguisorba minor*

Description   Salad Burnet is a perennial that grows in a neat round clump. Its size varies, as it is affected by the degree of richness of the soil. An average plant has a spread of 18in (45cm) and, when flowering, is 18in (45cm) high. The crimson and green flower balls are borne on long stalks, which emerge from the central clump.

Propagation   Salad burnet is easy to grow from seed but, as you may only need one or two plants, you may prefer to buy initially. It will self-seed readily.

Cultivation   It is an easy plant to grow and tolerant of most soils and conditions. It can be grown in a pot but is more suitable as a garden plant.

Uses   The leaves, each being divided into many tiny leaflets, taste faintly of cucumber. They can be stripped from the stems and added to salads and sandwiches instead of cress.

Savory, Summer *Satureja hortensis*

Description   Summer savory is a hardy annual. It is about 1ft (30cm) tall, bushy and has very small leaves and insignificant pale mauve flowers.

Propagation   As with most hardy annual herbs, it is easy to grow from seed. Sow in seed trays in early spring. As the seeds are very small, sow them as thinly as possible and take care not to cover too deeply. Thin out the seedlings in the tray, discarding the extra ones or, if you want a lot of plants, prick them out into further trays before planting out in their final positions. Summer savory can also be sown outside in April where it is to grow, thinning out as necessary. If this herb is grown in sufficient quantity surrounding a bean bed, it helps to reduce the incidence of blackfly on broad beans.

Savory, Winter *Satureja montana*

Description   Winter savory is the perennial version, and is a neat, compact plant, with denser growth than summer savory and small white flower spikes. If grown in rich soil, it will not have such a good flavour, but will make lusher growth and have more showy flowers.

Propagation   It can be propagated from seed. Alternatively, buy two or three plants to start

Fig 13   Summer savory enhances the flavour of beans and helps keep blackfly at bay.

Fig 14   Winter savory makes a neat edging plant. The flavour of both savories brings out the best in beans.

with and increase by cuttings or by dividing the plant in spring.

Cultivation for both savories   Native to the Mediterranean, savory grows well on a light, dry soil and needs plenty of sunshine. Winter savory is the one to grow for a container garden.

Uses for both savories   They have an affinity with all kinds of beans. The unusual, yet not overpowering flavour, of the savories makes them very versatile and they are used across a wide range of dishes from vegetable and egg to fish and meat.

Sorrel *Rumex acetosa*

Description   Also known as garden sorrel, this is a perennial which reaches 1ft 6in–2ft (45–60cm). The long, ovate acid-green leaves have a delectable fresh lemon flavour. They should be used when young. As the summer wears on, they tend to develop a stringy texture.

Varieties   There appears to be some confusion amongst authorities over the naming of sorrel. It is often claimed that 'French sorrel' is of superior flavour to the broadleaf garden variety, native to Britain. As far as I can discover, the plant referred to as French sorrel can either be a

20

specially selected strain of broadleaf sorrel, *Rumex acetosa* or buckler-leaved sorrel, *Rumex scutatus*, a low-growing, ground-cover sorrel with shield-shaped leaves.

Propagation   Sorrel can be grown from seed but, as a small supply is sufficient for most households, consider buying a plant or two initially, which can be increased by division in early spring.

Cultivation   It will tolerate most types of soil and a shaded position. In dry soil, it will run to seed more quickly. Keep snipping off flower spikes to encourage leafy growth.

Uses   Sorrel makes a light, lemony soup or, melted in butter and combined with fromage frais, an inimitable sauce for salmon or other oily fish.

Sweet Cicely *Myrrhis odorata*

Description   Sweet cicely is a perennial. The Latin name means 'fragrant perfume' and sweet cicely does have a sweet, delicate scent with overtones of aniseed. The light green, soft and feathery leaves are very decorative; the flower clusters are umbels of small white florets and are followed by distinctive long seed pods. Make sure you have the right plant as it bears a resemblance to 'fools' parsley', which is poisonous.

Sweet cicely spreads and gets bigger every year, growing to about 3ft 6in (1m). The whole plant dies down and disappears completely in

Fig 15   Sorrel is an easy plant to cultivate. Its fresh, lemon flavour is best enjoyed in spring when the leaves are young.

21

Fig 16   Sweet cicely. Make sure you get the right plant. It has feathery leaves and creamy-white flowers in early summer. Recognize it also by its distinctive seed-pods.

late autumn to re-emerge, fresh and green, in early spring or, if it is mild, as early as February.

Propagation   Once you have one sweet cicely plant, you are unlikely to need to propagate from it for your own use. It grows on a deep tap-root and is quite hard to get rid of as it regenerates from the root and also self-seeds readily. The seedlings are easy to transplant if you want to put some in a different place.

Cultivation   Little cultivation is needed. Sweet cicely will flourish in most soils and conditions, but prefers a well-drained, although not im-

poverished, soil. It is not a suitable plant for growing in pots.

Uses   Handfuls of the leaves cooked with gooseberries, or other tart soft fruits, bring out the flavour of the fruit, add a little sweetness and reduce acidity. The leaves also make a pretty garnish.

Tarragon *Artemisia dracunculus*

Description   French tarragon is the only kind worth growing for cooking; a perennial, it grows to about 2ft (60cm). The leaves are narrow and spear-shaped and grow on branching stems, arising from underground runners. The whole plant dies down in winter. French tarragon has a very distinctive flavour and scent. Do not con-fuse it with Russian tarragon which is a stronger-growing plant, larger and coarser, but virtually tasteless and, therefore, useless as a culinary herb.

Propagation   French tarragon cannot be prop-agated from seed. The easiest way to increase your stock is to divide the underground runners in spring. For guaranteed success, dig up a plant, put it in a large pot and overwinter in a green-house or under cover. In the spring, when you see new shoots coming through, turn the whole thing out of the pot and divide up the stem at each new shoot. Pot these up separately until they are strong enough to plant out.

Cultivation   A light, well-drained soil and sunny position is best for tarragon. Do not feed with manure or compost as this promotes lush growth which will detract from the flavour and make the plant less able to withstand cold conditions. Although it is reasonably hardy, tar-ragon does not always survive the winter if left in the ground. This is often because its roots become waterlogged. So, if your ground is not well-drained, dig up your tarragon plants and keep them in pots under cover through the winter. There could also be problems if the weather is very severe or the site very exposed. In these instances, if you do not wish to dig it up, cover the roots with straw or bracken to provide protection. Tarragon can be grown in containers but make sure you give it a big pot so that it has plenty of room to develop.

Uses   This is another first-choice herb. Its distinctive, strong yet subtle flavour complements chicken and fish and emphasizes the sweetness of carrots, parsnips or swedes.

Thyme *Thymus vulgaris* (common thyme)

Description   Thyme is a low-growing – up to 1ft (30cm) – shrubby perennial with tiny, tough, aromatic leaves and woody stems.

Varieties   There are many kinds of ornamental thymes but the one to use in the kitchen, apart from common thyme, is lemon thyme, *Thymus citriodorus*. The leaves are a brighter green and have a delicious lemon scent. It also has a neater habit of growth and gets less straggly than the common variety.

Propagation   Buy plants to start with and increase your stock, if required, from cuttings, root division or layering. Cuttings should be taken in April or May. Alternatively, dig up and divide the old plant in spring or autumn, or layer the side-shoots in early spring.

Cultivation   Thyme is a Mediterranean plant and is at its best in sunny dry conditions and not too rich a soil. Lemon thyme is less hardy than common thyme. All the thymes can suffer in the winter. They do not like to get water-logged, but a cold, biting wind seems to be their greatest enemy, so give them a winter coat of dried bracken or straw if they are in an exposed position. This is one of the few culinary herbs that can be allowed to flower without impairing the flavour of the leaves. It does tend to become very straggly. To counteract this, cut back after

flowering and renew the plants every three or four years. Thyme is an excellent subject for container growing.

Uses   Its strong, aromatic flavour makes thyme a good choice for adding to casseroles and dishes that need a long cooking process. It is an essential ingredient of bouquet garni.

Welsh Onion *Allium fistulosum*

Description   A perennial which grows to about 18in (45cm), it looks rather like giant chives with coarse hollow leaves. Tightly packed green

Fig 17   *Welsh onions look like giant chives. They are easy to grow in any soil and provide a ready source of green, onion-flavoured leaf.*

'bulbs', which break into greenish-white flower heads, appear on the stems in spring.

Propagation   As one or two plants are sufficient for most purposes, it is probably not worth the trouble of growing from seed. Buy in a plant and divide the roots, in early spring, to increase stocks as necessary. It will also self-seed.

Cultivation   Like most *alliums*, it does best in well-worked, reasonably rich soil, but is generally trouble-free to grow. It is not suitable for container growing.

Uses   It has onion-tasting leaves which can be chopped into salads or used to flavour soups, vegetables and egg dishes.

ORNAMENTAL AND FRAGRANT HERBS

The choice of plants suitable for the ornamental herb garden is a wide one. The following is not a definitive list, nor is it necessary to grow all those that are mentioned. They have been chosen to provide a reasonable selection for different purposes, schemes and situations and have been grouped accordingly under the headings below. As many are suitable for more than one purpose, there is some overlapping.

Herbs for Hedging and Knot Garden Work

Box	Cotton Lavender
Hyssop	Lavender
Rose	Rosemary
Rue	Wall Germander

Aromatic and Fragrant Herbs

Bergamot	Camomile
Costmary	Cotton Lavender
Curry Plant	Hyssop

Lavender	Lemon Balm
Lemon Verbena	Marjoram
Mint	Myrtle
Pennyroyal	Pinks
Rose	Rosemary
Rue	Sage
Scented-leaved	Southernwood
Pelargoniums	Thymes
Wormwood	

Herbs with Colourful Flowers

Blue   Borage, bugle, catmint.
Pink and Red   Bergamot, pineapple sage, pinks, rose, thyme.
Purple and Mauve   Lavender, marjoram, sage.
Yellow and Orange   Curry plant, cotton lavender, elecampane, lady's mantle, nasturtium, pot marigold, tansy.
White   Camomile, coriander, feverfew, myrtle, sweet cicely.

Herbs with Colourful Leaves

Purple and Bronze   Bronze fennel, bugle, purple basil, elder (*Sambucus purpurea*), purple sage, red orache.

Silver and Silvery Blue   Costmary, cotton lavender (*santolina*), curry plant, lavender, pinks, rue, sage, southernwood, thyme ('Silver Posie' and 'Silver Queen'), wormwood.

Gold and Variegated Gold/Green   Golden marjoram, gingermint, var. lemon balm, sage (*Icterina*), thyme (golden, golden lemon, 'Doone valley', *Nitidus*).

Variegated Cream/Green   Var. applemint (sometimes called pineapple mint), var. elder, var. rue, scented-leaved pelargoniums (*Crispum variegatum* and *Graveolens variegatum*).

Variegated Pink/Cream/Green   Sage (tricolor).

Variegated Pink/Cream/Mauve   Var. bugle.

Herbs for Special Situations

Tall Herbs Angelica, elecampane, fennel, lovage, red orache, rosemary.

Small Trees/Shrubs Bay, elder, myrtle.

Ground Cover Herbs Bugle, camomile ('Treneague'), corsican mint (*Mentha requienii*), pennyroyal (prostrate), thyme (creeping).

Herbs for Semi-Shade Angelica, bugle, feverfew, elecampane, lady's mantle, mint, pennyroyal, sweet cicely.

Herbs for Poor, Dry Soil Most of the silver-leaved herbs, tansy, soapwort (see Invasive Herbs).

Herbs for Damp Soil Angelica, bergamot, elecampane, mints, pennyroyal.

Angelica *Angelica archangelica*

(*See* the section on Culinary Herbs for more information.)

Description Angelica is a tall and statuesque plant that makes a worthy subject for the ornamental herb border.

Basil (Purple) *Ocimum purpurea*

(*See* the section on Culinary Herbs for more information.)

Description Purple basil can be used as a culinary herb, but its rich reddish-purple leaves and pink flower spikes equally earns it a place in the ornamental herb garden. It is best grown in a container.

Bay *Laurus nobilis*

(*See* the section on Culinary Herbs for more information.)

Description No herb garden should be without a bay. It makes an excellent container plant and lends itself very well indeed to ornamental clipping.

Bergamot *Monarda didyma*

Description Bergamot is a herbaceous perennial which grows to 3ft (90cm). The whole plant is fragrant and the pretty red, or pink, flowers, which appear in July or August, attract bees and butterflies, which are, of course, desirable visitors to a garden. The leaves are soft grey-green and downy to the touch.

Fig 18 Bergamot has glorious pink flowers which attract bees to the garden. Grow it in a damp situation.

Propagation   Buy plants to start with. To increase your stock, divide the roots in spring.

Cultivation   A damp soil, enriched with compost, and a partially shaded situation will suit bergamot best. It is not very suitable for container growing as it looks best massed in a border.

Uses   The flowers and leaves dry well and keep their fragrance, making them a useful addition to pot-pourri. One or two leaves can be added to the pot to give Indian tea a scented flavour.

Box *Buxus sempervirens*

Description   Left to itself, box becomes a large shrub but it is very slow-growing and can be kept trimmed to form the familiar box hedge. Box can be grown as a standard, or clipped to form spirals or pyramids. It is the traditional edging for herb gardens and is much used in knot garden work. It is an evergreen.

Varieties   For small hedges and edgings and for most knot garden designs, the dwarf variety, *Buxus sempervirens suffruticosa*, which grows to about 1ft 6 in (45cm), is the one to go for. There is also a gold and a variegated form of box with creamy margins to the leaves.

Propagation   If you just want a specimen plant as a feature, an interesting piece of topiary in a tub perhaps, then it is best to buy one ready-grown. But if you are planting a knot garden or extensive box edging, it will be very expensive to buy the requisite number of plants and you should consider propagating your own. However you will need to plan well ahead.

If you do not have access to any box, start by buying two or three stock plants and then take 3in (7.6cm) cuttings from them in August or September. Insert the cuttings around the edges of pots filled with mixed peat and sand (or a cuttings compost), and put them in a cold frame

or unheated greenhouse. Make sure they do not dry out, but do not keep them too wet either. There is no need to cover each pot with polythene. By the spring they should have rooted and will need more nutrients, so pot them up separately in a loam-based compost. Grow them on for two years, re-potting at the start of the second year, before planting out in September or October.

Cultivation   For a dense hedge, space the plants about 6in (15cm) apart. Remove one third of each leading shoot immediately after planting, to promote bushy growth. A box hedge will take moisture and goodness from the soil, so you will need to give extra water and a mulch of compost to herbs growing in proximity to it.

Bugle *Ajuga reptans*

Description   A traditional 'wound-herb', bugle makes an attractive ground cover plant. It is a perennial which grows on a creeping root-stock and has bright blue flower spikes in spring. It grows to about 6in (15cm).

Varieties   *A. r. purpurea* has deep purple leaves. There is also an unusual multicoloured form.

Propagation   Start by buying in a plant. It will soon spread and is easy to propagate by separating off-shoots and re-planting them elsewhere.

Cultivation   As it is a woodland plant in its wild state, bugle grows well in shady situations. It needs to be kept reasonably moist. For container growing, bugle looks effective in a mixed ornamental tub.

Camomile

Description   This has several forms, but they are often all referred to simply as 'camomile'. As they have quite different characteristics, this can be confusing for the new herb gardener.

Fig 19 Bugle (Ajuga reptans).

Roman Camomile *Anthemis nobilis*   This is a perennial on a creeping root-stock, whose flower stalks grow to about 1ft 6in (45cm). It has single, yellow-centred daisy flowers. If intended as a carpeting herb, it will need constant clipping from May onwards to prevent it flowering.

Treneague Camomile *Anthemis nobilis* 'Treneague'   This is the non-flowering form which is best for camomile lawns. As these lawns are not as easy to establish and maintain as is sometimes claimed, a patch of camomile amongst the paving stones on the patio makes an attractive and more manageable alternative. Treneague is also suitable for camomile seats.

Double-Flowered Camomile *Anthemis nobilis flora plena*   This is a very pretty version with round, creamy buttons of flowers that dry well. It is a neater, more compact plant than the other flowering camomiles and much lower-growing, at 3–4in (7–10cm). It also needs a richer soil and more water.

German Camomile *Matricaria chamomilla* This one is an annual. It has single, white, yellow-centred, daisy flowers in midsummer. It grows to about 2ft (60cm) and suits a mixed border, but cannot be grown as a carpeting herb.

Characteristics of all Camomiles   The foliage smells of sweet apples, a scent which is intensified by rain and released by crushing the plant. It is often said that camomile is a low-growing plant. However, although the foliage is low-growing, the flower stems are not. Only the dwarf, double-flowered variety makes a good edging plant if allowed to flower. If growing camomile for the flowers, do not be tempted to put the single-flowered Roman camomile or the annual camomile at the front of the border.

Propagation   The perennials are easy to propagate from offsets and runners in the spring. Annual camomile is propagated from seed.

Cultivation   The taller-growing camomiles become rather sprawling as summer progresses. Once they have flowered, cut them right back to keep untidiness in check. The camomiles have a preference for a light, sandy soil, but they are easy plants to cultivate. The perennial forms can be grown effectively in garden tubs.

27

Fig 20   Catmint, Nepeta musinii, *looks best in a mass planting and flowers over a long period from early to midsummer.*

Uses   An infusion of the flowers makes a rinse to add lustre to fair hair. Camomile tea, made from the fresh or dried flowers, is a soothing bed-time drink and is also beneficial for digestive upsets.

Catmint *Nepeta mussinii*

Description   Catmint is a perennial, which grows to 1ft–1ft 6in (30–45cm) tall. It is the garden variety of *Nepeta cataria* or catnip, and is a prettier, less sprawling, plant. It has grey leaves and misty-blue flowers throughout the summer and makes a wonderful show in a mass planting.

Propagation   It can be grown from seed, or

you could buy a few plants initially, which can be increased by dividing the roots in spring.

Cultivation   This is an easy plant to grow in any soil. Catmint looks its best in a mass planting and does not make a good container plant.

Coriander *Coriandrum sativum*

(See the section on Culinary Herbs for more information.)

Description   Although primarily a culinary herb, the profusion of white flowers and feathery leaves in midsummer make coriander an equally good choice for an ornamental scheme.

Fig 21   Costmary, also known as 'Bible Leaf' makes a fragrant bookmark. Introduced to Britain in the sixteenth century, it does not set seed there but spreads freely on its creeping root system.

Costmary *Tanacetum balsamita*

Description   Costmary is also called 'alecost' – a reference to its earlier use in brewing. A perennial, it grows to 2ft (60cm). The large, flat, bluish-grey leaves have a light balsam fragrance. They were often used as bookmarks in church, hence another of its folk names – Bible Leaf. The yellow flowers are insignificant.

Propagation   This is a plant to buy. It is unlikely that you will want to propagate it as it grows on a creeping root-stock and spreads but, should you decide to do so, take cuttings from the roots as you would for mint.

Cultivation   Costmary will grow in most types of soil. It is not a good container plant.

Cotton Lavender *Santolina chamaecyparissus*

Description   Cotton lavender is no relation to lavender, despite its common name. It is a perennial which grows to about 1ft 6in (45cm) and keeps its foliage throughout the winter. It has decorative silver-grey leaves, which smell of moth balls, and bright yellow button flowers in midsummer. Cotton lavender looks good in mixed ornamental containers.

Fig 23   Cotton lavender, Santolina, *has finely divided decorative foliage and is a traditional knot garden herb.*

Fig 22   Coriander is a popular culinary herb when grown for the leaves and seeds, but the feathery foliage and pretty white flowers earn it a place in the ornamental herb garden as well.

Varieties   *Santolina viridis*, which has feathery greeny-gold foliage, makes a pretty contrast to the silver-leaved form.

Propagation   Take cuttings in late summer, inserting them in a cuttings compost. Keep the cuttings in a cold frame or greenhouse until they have rooted, then pot them up separately to grow on before planting them the following spring. Cuttings can also be taken in spring for autumn planting.

Cultivation   A sunny situation and a light soil is best for this easy-to-grow plant. Cotton lavender was introduced to Britain in the sixteenth-century as a hedging plant for knot gardens. When grown as a dwarf hedge, it needs frequent clipping to prevent flowering. Single plants will benefit from ruthless clipping if they are not to grow leggy and straggly.

Uses It is well known for its insect repellent properties. The leaves can be dried for inclusion in scented sachets.

Curry Plant *Helichrysum angustifolium*

Description So named because its spicy smell is reminiscent of curry, this is a shrubby, silver-leaved perennial with bright yellow flowers. The curry plant keeps its leaves through the winter but, in very cold or exposed areas, it is liable to suffer and may not survive.

Propagation Take cuttings in August or early September. They should root within a few weeks, when they can be potted up separately, in a loam-based compost. Keep them under cover through the winter and they will be ready to plant out in the spring.

Cultivation Curry plant likes a free-draining soil and sunny position. Cut it back after it has flowered. Plants may need replacing every few years because they tend to become straggly. This is another herb to put in a mixed ornamental container.

Elder *Sambucus nigra*

Description Once known as 'the poor man's medicine chest', since it is 'useful in all its parts', this familiar deciduous tree of roadside and hedgerow is now all too often despised as a 'weed'. This is a pity as the creamy, scented flower-heads and glistening black berries have many uses.

Varieties The common elder is inclined to seed itself in awkward places and can become difficult to eradicate once it has become established. Therefore, if you prefer to obtain your supplies of flowers and berries from the wild, consider growing some of the less invasive ornamental elders in the herb garden; they make attractive screening plants:

Fig 24 *Elecampane is a tall plant, suited to the back of the border. The cheerful, golden flower-heads are borne in midsummer.*

Sambucus albo variegata has dark green leaves edged with cream.
S. aureus has golden leaves.
S. laciniata has finely divided, fern-like leaves.
S. purpurea has dramatic, dark purple leaves.

Propagation Should you desire to do so, the common elder is easy to propagate from a sucker or cutting taken from a wild plant. Buy the more fancy varieties from a specialist nursery and take cuttings from them in spring or summer.

Cultivation Common elder is undemanding. The best conditions for the others are a damp, fertile soil and sunny position. To keep a neat shape and check growth, prune all elders in their dormant period (November–January). Elders are not for containers.

Uses The flowers make wines and cordials, flavour sweets and sorbets, and add a muscatel flavour to gooseberries. An infusion of elder-flowers makes a toning lotion for dry, sensitive skins. The berries also make excellent wines and cordials as well as chutneys, preserves and elderberry and apple pie.

Elecampane *Inula helenium*

Description   This ancient medicinal plant is a tall perennial that grows to about 5ft (1.5m). It has big, bold leaves and bright-golden daisylike flowers which bloom in midsummer.

Propagation   This is a herb for the larger garden and should be planted in clumps at the back of a border. One plant on its own is not worth growing. Sow seeds in spring; they can be slow to germinate. It can also be propagated by taking off-sets from the roots in autumn.

Cultivation   A moist soil and a semi-shaded position provide ideal conditions for growing this plant. It is not a suitable subject for container growing.

Fennel *Foeniculum vulgare*

(See the section on Culinary Herbs for more information.)

Description   Both green and bronze fennel make striking ornamental plants.

Feverfew *Chrysanthemum parthenium*, also known as *Tanacetum parthenium*

Description   Feverfew is a short-lived perennial, said to be effective against migraine attacks. It has pretty, daisy-like flowers, growing to 2ft (60cm) from clumps of strong, not very pleasant-smelling, much-divided leaves.

Varieties   There is a golden-leaved form that has more attractive foliage but not, apparently, the same medicinal properties. There is also a double-flowered variety.

Propagation   Feverfew is easy to grow from seed and, once in the garden, self-seeds proli-

Fig 25   *Feverfew is an easy plant to grow. This double-flowered form is an attractive alternative to the more common variety.*

fically. However, it is not difficult to control, unlike plants with deep tap-roots. Pull out unwanted seedlings as they appear. Feverfew will grow in any soil. It is not a very suitable container plant.

Hyssop *Hyssopus officinalis*

Description   Hyssop is a perennial small shrub, or 'sub-shrub', and has long been a traditional dwarf hedging herb. It has small, dark green, spice-scented leaves and rich-blue flower spikes in August. There are also pink and white-flowered hyssops. It can grow to 2ft (60cm) but can be clipped back to keep it shorter. In a mild winter it is evergreen but in severe weather it loses many of its leaves.

Propagation   It is easy to grow from seed. This is a convenient method of propagating it if a number of plants are needed for a hedge or knot garden. In order to perpetuate a particular flower colour, take cuttings, removing each one at a leaf joint.

Cultivation   An ordinary garden soil, plenty of sunshine and a sheltered situation are perfect for this generally undemanding plant. Cut it back to keep it trim and re-plant after about four years if it becomes leggy. For a close-growing hedge, plant at 9in (23cm) intervals.

Uses   (See Culinary Herb section.)

Fig 26 Lady's mantle, Alchemilla mollis, *holds a diamond dew-drop in the centre of each fan-shaped leaf. Alchemists of old believed these had magical properties.*

Lady's mantle *Alchemilla mollis*

Description Lady's mantle is a herbaceous perennial which grows to about 1ft (30cm) high, and was once widely used as a medicinal herb. The name is a reference to its sixteenth-century association with the Virgin Mary, its pleated leaves being thought to resemble a mantle. Of spreading, but not untidy, habit, the decorative foliage and profusion of greenish-yellow flowers make it a welcome herb garden plant.

Propagation Buy a plant to start with. Once established, it will spread and self-seed. Pull out unwanted plants as they appear and re-position.

Cultivation Any ordinary, well-drained soil is suitable and a semi-shaded position ideal. It is more suited to growing in the garden than in pots.

Lavender *Lavandula* species

Traditional English lavender is a hardy perennial, which grows to about 2ft 6in (75cm) and has silver-grey spiky foliage and the familiar mauve-blue highly scented flowers. There are many forms which are known variously, in botanical terms, as *Lavandula angustifolia, L. officinalis, L. spica,* and *L. vera.* The plants offered for sale under the banner of lavender or English lavender are as various and muddled as the nomenclature. To make sure you are getting what you expect, try to see the plant in flower before buying.

If you go for one of the named cultivars, you can be sure of getting the plant you bargained for. The two top favourites are 'Dwarf Munstead', a compact plant growing to 1ft (30cm) with lavender-blue flowers, and 'Hidcote', which is a little taller at 1ft 6in (45cm) and has the inimitable deep-purple flowers. *Lavandula stoechas,* sometimes called French lavender, is an unusual and attractive variety, the purple flower bracts being larger than more traditional lavenders. *L. stoechas* grows in a neat clump to about 1ft 6in (45cm). In northern areas of Britain it may not be completely hardy.

Propagation Lavender can be grown from seed but, to get a plant which is true to its parent, propagate from cuttings. Pull pieces off the stem with a 'heel' attached. Insert these in a sandy cuttings compost in pots or trays and keep them on a window-sill or in the greenhouse until they have rooted. Pot them up separately in a loam-based compost – soilless all-purpose composts hold too much moisture for young lavender plants. Keep them under protection through the winter and plant them out the following spring.

Cultivation Lavender cannot tolerate a heavy, clay soil. Give it a free-draining soil and an open, sunny position and it will thrive. Once it has flowered (which will be by the end of August), rather than just removing flower stems, cut it back hard to prevent the bush becoming straggly and to encourage new growth the following year. Some of the lower-growing species of lavender look very well in pots.

Uses Well-known for its use in lavender bags, pot-pourris and other scented articles, lavender also has antiseptic and insect-repellent properties.

Lemon Balm *Melissa officinalis*

See the section on Culinary Herbs for more information.)

Description Variegated lemon balm is most suitable for the ornamental herb garden, making a lovely splash of gold.

Cultivation Grow it in full sun and cut it well back if it shows signs of reverting to a plain leaf.

Fig 27 Variegated lemon balm makes a bright splash of colour and is not as invasive as the common variety.

Fig 28 Originally a South American plant, and not completely hardy, lemon verbena can be grown outside throughout the year in a sheltered position in the warm, temperate climates – as seen here in the scented garden at Hatfield House, Hertfordshire.

Lemon Verbena *Aloysia triphylla* (or *Lippia citriodora*)

Description This fragrant, lemon-scented plant is a deciduous shrub, originating from South America, and not to be confused with that homely member of the mint family, lemon balm, *Melissa officinalis*. It has rough-textured, spear-shaped leaves and rather insignificant mauve-white flowers, borne on racemes at the stem-ends. In temperate climates, under favourable conditions, lemon verbena may reach 6–8ft

33

(1.8–2.4m), but I have seen it grown in New Zealand, unchecked by hard frost, to form a dense 15ft (4.5m) high hedge.

Propagation   Lemon verbena is not very easy for the home gardener to propagate. It is slow to root and the developing plant requires heat throughout the winter.

Cultivation   It is not completely hardy. It will tolerate some degree of frost – supposedly to −5°C (23°F) – but it will not take kindly to long periods of sub-zero temperatures, nor withstand temperatures below −5°C (23°F) at all. Therefore, it can be grown outside in southern Britain, but a sheltered site against a south-facing wall is advisable, and be prepared to lose some plants if winters turn severe.

To be on the safe side, grow lemon verbena in large pots or tubs, which can be moved to the shelter of a frost-free greenhouse in winter. A loam-based compost will suit it best. In the summer, you will need to give pot-grown subjects an occasional liquid feed and keep them well-watered. In the autumn, cut back the branches to about half their length to encourage bushy growth for the next season; the fresh shoots appear in April or May. Give a minimum of water through the winter months when the plant is dormant.

Uses   Lemon verbena is high in essential oil content and the dried leaves retain their fragrance for years. Therefore, they are ideal for use in pot-pourris and scented bags. The fresh or dried leaves also make a delicious and refreshing tea.

Lovage *Levisticum officinalis*

(See the section on Culinary Herbs for more information.)

Description   Although not a particularly decorative plant, lovage can be useful to provide height in a scheme.

Marigold, Pot *Calendula officinalis*

Description   The old-fashioned English pot marigold is an annual which grows to 1ft–1ft 6in (30–45cm). The bright orange-yellow blooms provide colour and a brilliant foil for green-leaved herbs, throughout the summer.

Propagation   They are easy to grow from seed, sown directly into the ground in April, or started off a little earlier in seed trays for transplanting in April or May. Pot marigolds self-seed prolifically.

Cultivation   Pot marigolds are easy to grow and thrive in any soil, including the poorest. They will do best in a sunny position. Remove the dead heads to ensure continuous flowering throughout the summer. If grown in pots, plant close together and do not feed as this will encourage leaf at the expense of flowers.

Uses   Once an important medicinal herb, pot marigold petals have healing properties and are still used to make soothing ointments for chapped skin. The dried flowers add colour and interest to pot-pourri.

(See the section on Culinary Herbs for uses in cookery.)

Marjoram, Golden *Origanum aureum*

Description   This is a perennial with greeny-gold leaves. The new growth each year forms a compact cushion. To preserve this effect cut back the flower stems as they appear. Flowers are white. There is also an attractive variegated form whose green leaves are tipped with gold.

Propagation   Dig up the clumps in autumn or spring, divide the roots and replant. Marjoram spreads so you will need to do this anyway to keep it tidy. One plant soon forms into a fair-sized clump.

Cultivation Golden marjoram is grown for the glory of the foliage and, if allowed to flower it will sprawl, so for maximum effect keep it well trimmed. It can be used as an edging, when it should be planted at 6–8in (15–20cm) intervals. A fairly rich soil and a sunny sheltered position will suit it best. It can be grown in containers.

Mint *Mentha* species

Description There are several kinds of mint which are indispensable to a fragrant or ornamental herb garden. Top of the list are:

Variegated Applemint *Mentha rotundifolia variegata* This is a neat-growing mint with cream and green variegated leaves.

Eau-De-Cologne Mint This is a form of *Mentha citrata*, also known as bergamot mint. It has smooth-textured, round leaves, tinged with bronze, and a delightful fresh fragrance.

Gingermint *Mentha gentilis* This is another variegated mint with acid-green leaves slashed with gold.

Corsican Mint *Mentha requienii* This is a very low-growing ground cover plant with tiny leaves.

Fig 29 The striking foliage of variegated applemint makes it a first choice for the ornamental herb garden.

Propagation From stem cuttings, as for the culinary mints already described. None of these mints breed true from seed.

Cultivation All the mints need a damp well-composted soil. They make good container plants.

Uses Eau-de-cologne mint can be dried for pot-pourri, or put in a draw-string bag to scent the bath water.

Myrtle *Myrtus communis*

Description Myrtle is an evergreen shrub and grows 6–7ft (1.8–2.1m) tall. The aromatic leaves are a dark, glossy green. It has round white flowers in midsummer, followed by blue-black berries.

Varieties There are variegated and double-flowered forms of myrtle and a very attractive dwarf variety, *Myrtus communis 'Tarentina'*, which is a good one for a container garden.

Propagation Buy myrtle plants to start with. They are not the easiest of plants to propagate being slow to root. If you want to try, take heel cuttings in September, dip the ends in hormone-rooting powder, insert in potting compost and keep in a cold frame, or on the kitchen window-sill, until they have rooted, which will be in the following spring. Pot them up in a loam-based compost and grow them on for at least a year, re-potting as necessary, before attempting to plant out.

Cultivation Myrtle is not a reliably hardy plant, although in a sheltered site in temperate climates it may survive outside. The double-flowered variety will definitely not tolerate frost. To be on the safe side, grow myrtle in a pot, in a loam-based compost, keeping it outside in the summer and under shelter, protected from frost through the winter.

Fig 30 Myrtus communis tarentina *(in the terra-cotta pot) is a dwarf form of myrtle. The leaves can be dried for inclusion in pot-pourris.*

Uses Myrtle is dedicated to Venus and a sprig was traditionally included in a bridal bouquet. The dried leaves add fragrance to pot-pourri.

Nasturtium *Tropaeolum majus*

Description Introduced from South America, by way of France and Flanders, in the late sixteenth century, this brightly coloured annual has been popular ever since. Not all of them are hardy.

Varieties There are trailing and more compact forms, both have creeping foliage.

Propagation Seeds germinate easily. They can be sown in spring in the open where they are required to flower.

Cultivation An open, sunny position and well-drained soil is best for nasturtiums. A too fertile soil will encourage leaf growth at the expense of flowers. Nasturtiums grow well in tubs, the trailing ones are suitable for tall pots and hanging baskets.

Uses See the section on Culinary Herbs for uses in cookery.

Orache, Red *Atriplex hortensis rubra*

Description Red orache is a tall and skinny hardy annual, growing to about 4ft (1.2m). It does not spread far sideways. It is worth growing for its striking dark red foliage and decorative seed heads.

Propagation One plant looks rather lost so, in order to have enough for a group, grow it from seed sown directly into the ground in April. It can also be raised in seed trays for certainty of germination. You could start by buying two or three plants as it will usually self-seed to provide plants for the following year. For the maximum effect, grow it in groups at the back of the border, or at strategic intervals, to give height to a scheme.

Cultivation It is an easy-going plant, which tolerates relatively poor, stony soil. But for lush growth and to achieve its maximum height it will need more fertile conditions, provided by adding compost and by giving it extra watering. It is not a suitable plant for container growing.

Uses In its common or garden green-leaved form, it was once widely grown as a pot herb. Although it is not worth growing red orache principally as a culinary herb, the leaves are edible and make an unusual garnish.

Pelargoniums, Scented-Leaved *Pelargonium* species

Description Often referred to as 'scented geraniums', they are of the same genus as the familiar pelargoniums, with large red or pink flowers, still known to many people as 'geraniums'. The scented-leaved varieties, many of which were introduced to Britain in the eighteenth century, have comparatively insignificant flowers and are grown for the fragrance and interest of the foliage.

Varieties   There are many to choose from and a specialist nursery would provide a full list. Some of the most popular are:
Graveolens   This is often referred to as 'rose geranium' but in fact the scent is nearer to lemons than roses.
Crispum and *Crispum variegatum*   These are also lemon-scented.
Tomentosum   This has broad, bright green, downy leaves, smelling of peppermint. (It was one of the earliest to be introduced in Britain, in 1710.)
Fragrans   This has silvery-green foliage and a scent of pine.

Propagation   Most of the pelargoniums take well from cuttings. Late summer is the best time to try them. Insert cuttings in a loam-based compost in pots. Cover each pot with a polythene bag to preserve moisture and make sure they are kept in the shade until rooted. Pot up individually and keep indoors, or in a heated greenhouse, through the winter.

Cultivation   Scented-leaved pelargoniums are best grown in containers to stand outside during the summer months and moved into a frost-free environment during the winter. Water well through the summer and give an occasional liquid feed. Cut them back in the autumn and allow them to rest through the winter, by not feeding and watering sparingly. They make lovely fragrant house-plants.

Uses   The leaves can be used both in cookery to flavour cakes and custards, and dried in potpourris to add fragrance, hence the popularity of this plant.

Pennyroyal *Mentha pulegium*

Description   A member of the mint family, pennyroyal has a pleasing, fresh scent and neat foliage. There is a creeping – 4in (10cm) – and an upright – 1ft (30cm) – form. The former is useful for ground cover, making a dense sweet-smelling carpet. Both varieties have pale purple flowers grown in whorls round the stems.

Propagation   As with other mints, pennyroyal has underground runners which can be lifted, cut into sections and replanted.

Cultivation   It needs a damp soil to thrive, so keep it well watered. It will grow happily in shade. Provided the soil is not too dry, the low-growing form is ideal for growing around paving slabs to soften the edges. Pennyroyal could be container-grown.

Uses   Once used to sweeten stale drinking water, pennyroyal also has a reputation as an insect repellent, as its Latin name implies (pulegium comes from pulex, which is the Latin word for flea).

Pinks *Dianthus* species

Description   The traditional herb garden form of dianthus is the clove carnation, *Dianthus caryophyllus*, but any of the members of this large and varied genus could be included in an ornamental herb garden. Pinks are highly suitable for mixed ornamental tubs and pots.

Propagation   They are not difficult to grow from cuttings taken in late summer, or by layering after flowering is finished.

Cultivation   Plant in a sunny position in well-drained soil.

Uses   The flowers can be dried for pot-pourris and can also be used as a decorative garnish in cookery.

Rose *Rosa* species

Roses were at one time popularly believed to have valuable medicinal properties and they have always had their place in the herb garden. The old-fashioned varieties are most in keeping. One of the oldest and most traditional for the purpose is:

'The Apothecary's Rose' *Rosa gallica officinalis*

Description   It has bright pink, semi-double blooms, which open out flat to reveal a mass of golden stamens. A shrub rose of compact form, growing to about 4ft × 4ft (1.2m × 1.2m), it flowers only once a year, usually at the end of June and beginning of July.

Varieties   There are several other types of gallica rose, including 'Rosa mundi' *R. gallica versicolour*, a striped pink and white version, and 'Tuscany superb', which has dramatic, densely petalled dark crimson blooms and a delightful perfume.

Cultivation   A generous mulch of compost or manure in early spring should keep these roses in good heart, along with a sprinkling of proprietary rose food, forked into the soil, as they come into bud. Shrub roses do not need hard pruning; all that is needed is to keep them trimmed into a neat shape.

Uses   Roses form the basis of most pot-pourris. An infusion of the petals makes an effective toning lotion for a sensitive skin. The blooms can also be used in a variety of ways in cookery. (See the section on Culinary Herbs for more information.)

Rosemary *Rosmarinus officinalis*

Rosemary is as important to the ornamental as to the culinary garden. (See the section on Culinary Herbs for further details.)

Rue *Ruta graveolens*

Description   This strong-smelling shrubby perennial has decoratively divided blue-green leaves and is usually evergreen, although older plants often lose most of their leaves in winter. It grows about 1ft 6in–2ft (45cm–60cm) and has greeny-yellow flowers in summer. Ask for 'Jackman's Blue', a cultivar with steel-blue leaves.

Propagation   One or two rue plants would be enough for most purposes, in which case it is best to buy them. However, if you want to grow rue in greater quantity, as an edging or low hedge, for example, you will need to propagate your own. Ordinary rue can be grown from seed but 'Jackman's Blue' will need to be propagated from cuttings taken in late summer. They will root in three to four weeks, when they should be potted up and kept in a frame or cold greenhouse through the winter before planting out the following spring. If you start seeds off in March or early April, they will be ready for planting out by the end of June. A word of warning: rue can cause nasty blisters if the skin brushes against it, so always wear gloves to take cuttings and handle plants.

Cultivation   Rue needs good drainage and will tolerate a poor soil. It can be kept trimmed to make neat round cushions for an effective edge or front of border. Rue can be grown in containers.

Uses   Rue has a very strong, almost unpleasant, odour, and is one of the herbs that in former times was included in the judge's posy to protect him from gaol fever.

Sage *Salvia* species

There are several forms of sage to include in an ornamental and fragrant herb garden:

Purple Sage (*S.o. 'Purpurescens'* This has dark purple and green leaves, and *S.o. 'Icterina'*, [1ft

Fig 31   Rue will grow happily in shade. Here it is beneath an avenue of lime trees at Barnsley House, Gloucestershire.

Fig 32   Icterina (right) and purple sage (left) with silvery-blue curry plant.

(30cm)], has golden variegated leaves. *S.o. 'Trico-lor'* [1ft 6in (45cm)] has leaves splashed with cream, pink and green and is less hardy, needing some protection from frost and severe weather. These three forms are evergreen perennials.

Pineapple Sage *S. rutilans* This grows to 3ft (90cm) and is a tender plant which must be kept frost-free. Grow it in a large pot to stand outside in the summer. The leaves have a delicious, pineapple scent. In autumn, bright-red flower-spikes appear.

Clary Sage *S. Sclarea* This grows to 3ft 6in (1m) and is a hardy biennial. It is worth growing for its spectacular flower spikes in subtle combinations of pink, blue and white.

Propagation With the exception of clary sage, which should be propagated from seed, the coloured-leaved sages must be increased by cuttings or layering. The easiest one to propagate is pineapple sage. Take cuttings from the fleshy stems, just below a leaf joint. Insert into a cuttings compost, keep moist, and almost every one will root within a matter of days.

Cultivation All the sages prefer a well-drained soil and a sunny situation. Pineapple sage needs a great deal of water, especially if pot-grown, when its roots will be restricted. If you do neglect it and it wilts, do not despair, just turn the hose on it and the stems will suck up the water as if through a drinking straw. The ornamental sages can all be pot grown. Clary sage is not suitable.

Soapwort *Saponaria officinalis*

(See the section on Invasive Herbs.)

Southernwood *Artemisia abrotanum*

Description This feathery, clean-smelling herb

Fig 33   Southernwood Artemisia abrotanum *(in the centre of the picture behind the lavender) is easy to grow from cuttings.*

is known by a variety of common names, including 'Old Man' and 'Lad's Love'. The French know it as 'Garde Robe', a reference to its insect repellent properties, as it was laid among clothes in the wardrobe to keep moths at bay.

A shrubby perennial which grows to about 3ft 6in (1m), it keeps most of its grey-green foliage through the winter if the weather is not too severe, although older plants may not do so. It makes an attractive low-growing hedge.

Propagation This is one of the easiest herbs to increase by cuttings, although you may wish to buy a plant or two to start you off. Take cuttings either from the soft new growth or from the woodier stems from May through to July. Insert into a standard 'cuttings compost' and roots will form in two to three weeks.

Pot up rooted cuttings individually and plant out in early autumn or, in colder areas especially, overwinter and plant out in spring. Cuttings will also take if put straight into a garden bed if kept well-watered and lightly shaded.

Cultivation Southernwood is a Mediterranean plant and a light, free-draining soil and sunshine suit it best. It needs hard trimming to keep it in shape and prevent it becoming woody and straggly at the base. In northern areas of Britain, where it is more likely to be adversely affected by cold winters, it can be cut back almost to ground level in spring to encourage it into bushy new growth. Southernwood is not very suitable for container-growing.

Uses   Southernwood can be dried to add to a pot-pourri, or to put into sachets to keep in the wardrobe or linen cupboard to deter moths and insects.

Sweet Cicely *Myrrhis odorata*

Description   Although primarily listed as a culinary herb, there is a place for this in the ornamental garden. It is a useful plant for a shady situation or to fill an awkward corner where nothing seems to flourish. (*See* the section on Culinary Herbs for more information.)

Tansy *Tanacetum vulgare*

(*See* the section on Invasive Herbs.)

Thymes *Thymus* species

The range and variety of foliage and flowers amongst the different forms of thyme make this group of plants invaluable in the ornamental herb garden. They are all perennial evergreens and can be divided into two main groups:

Upright and Bushy Thymes

These are like miniature shrubs, and range from 5in–1ft (12–30cm) in height:

Golden *Thymus vulgaris aureus*   This grows to 5in (12cm). Its leaves turn bright gold when planted in full sun. The flowers are pink.

Golden Lemon *Thymus x citriodorus aureus* This grows to 6in (15cm). It has gold/green variegated leaves, pink flowers and a lovely lemon scent.

Nitidus *Thymus nitidus*   This grows to 6in (15cm). It is a white-flowered thyme with gold-green foliage.

Silver Posy *Thymus vulgaris variegata*   This grows to 6in (15cm). It has silver, variegated leaves and pink flowers.

Silver Queen *Thymus x citriodorus variegata* This grows to 6in (15cm). It is lemon-scented, but a slightly less attractive version of Silver Posy.

Creeping and Spreading Thymes

These are suitable for ground cover:

Albus *Thymus serpyllum album*   This grows to 2in (5cm). It forms a mat of tiny green leaves with white flowers.

Annie Hall *Thymus Annie Hall*   This grows to 2in (5cm). It has bright green spiky leaves and pink flowers.

Coccineus Major *Thymus coccineus major*   This grows to 2in (5cm). It has dark glossy green leaves and rich crimson flowers.

Herba Barona *Thymus herba barona*   This grows to 2in (5cm). It has strands of shiny green leaves which are caraway-scented and flowers of a deep rose-purple.

Lanuginosus *Thymus lanuginosus*   This grows to 2in (5cm). The grey, woolly leaves form a dense mat and the flowers are pale mauve.

Pink Chintz *Thymus Pink Chintz*   This grows to 4in (10cm). It has grey-green foliage, which is slightly hairy, and clear pink flowers.

Russetings *Thymus Russetings*   This grows to 4in (10cm). It has dark green foliage and purple flowers.

Propagation   Buy named varieties of all these thymes and increase them if you need to by taking cuttings. This can be done at any time during the summer months. Cut non-flowering shoots about 1in (3cm) long, put them in pots or trays filled with a peat and sand mixture and, when they have rooted, pot them up and plant out when strong and bushy.

Cultivation   Thymes hate to be cold and wet. Grow them in free-draining soil in a sunny position. They do not always survive cold winters, usually because they become water-logged or are exposed to cold, biting winds. Sometimes they will regenerate if the damaged growth is cut back hard. All thymes need regular trimming and most will need replacing after three to four years when they become straggly. They make excellent subjects for pots.

Wall Germander *Teucrium chamaedrys*

Description An evergreen perennial with shiny, dark green oak-leaf foliage, and pinky-purple flower spikes in July and August. It grows to 1ft 6in (45cm).

Traditionally a knot garden herb, it can be kept trimmed to form a low-growing hedge or border edge.

Propagation It is easy to grow from cuttings, or by division of the creeping roots in autumn. Start with a stock plant and take cuttings any time throughout the summer, starting in May or June. Cuttings can be put straight into a garden bed if kept well watered and lightly shaded. To form a thick, low hedge, plant at 6in (15cm) intervals and keep well trimmed as it grows.

Cultivation It is an undemanding plant which will grow in almost any soil, including the poorest. It is not recommended as a container plant.

Wormwood *Artemisia absinthum*

Description A pretty silver-leaved shrub, with deeply cut foliage, wormwood has a bitter scent which helps to keep insects away. It is a perennial that can grow to 4ft (1.2m) and has tiny, insignificant greenish-yellow flowers.

Propagation You will probably only need one or two plants in the herb garden, so it makes sense to buy. It grows on a creeping root system, so if you do want to increase your stock it is a simple matter to divide the roots, digging up and replanting new shoots in spring.

Cultivation Wormwood will grow in most soils and tolerates shade well. Once the flowers appear it becomes straggly-looking and should be cut back almost to base, when it will sprout again and produce fresh growth. It is not very suitable for growing in containers.

INVASIVE HERBS

The ease with which herbs grow is an undoubted advantage; it can also be their main disadvantage, as a few can be tiresomely persistent. Many herbs, especially some of the traditional medicinal ones, are wild plants. In certain circumstances, when they spring up uncultivated and unwanted, they could be considered 'weeds'. After all, ground elder, known as 'bishop's goutweed', was once a prized medicinal plant.

Many more herbs than are listed here may spread or self-seed but most are not too difficult to control. The ones given below are the sort that are not easy to keep in check or to eradicate once established. This is not to say they should never be seen in a garden, some have a very useful part to play but, before planting any of them, consider whether you could take steps to contain them by means of brick or tile divisions, and make sure that where you first plant them is where you want them to stay. If you are very short of space, it is probably better to go for some of the less rapacious and more attractive plants.

Comfrey *Symphytum officinalis*

Description Comfrey is a large plant, growing to over 3ft (90cm) and spreading as far across. Once it has finished flowering it is not particularly attractive. It spreads and self-seeds and as it regenerates from a deep tap-root system is almost impossible to eradicate. In fact the more you dig it up, the stronger it grows and the more it proliferates.

Uses Despite the problems, it has much in its favour. It is useful for home remedies. One of its country names is 'knitbone' and it contains 'allantoin', a recognized healing agent. A poultice of the leaves (softened in boiling water) really does reduce swellings and soothes cuts and bruises. The leaves also make an excellent compost heap activator and organic fertilizer. Grow it if you have the space but in an obscure corner and not as the centre-piece of an elegant scheme you may later want to change.

Good King Henry *Chenopodium bonus-henricus*

Description This perennial is a fairly low-growing – to about 1ft 6in (45cm) – spreading herb with arrow-shaped, dark green leaves and greeny-yellow flower spikes in spring. It is a wild plant which grows easily in any soil and flourishes in salty, windy areas, such as by the sea. It is also known as Mercury and Fat Hen, a reference to its poultry-fattening propensities, as it contains steroids.

Uses Although inclined to take over, it is a

Fig 34   Good King Henry is a nourishing but invasive alternative to spinach.

useful herb for filling an awkward corner in the herb garden, making good ground cover as no weeds grow through it and it is tolerant of shade and dry conditions. The young leaves are a spinach substitute.

Horse-radish *Cochlearia armoracia*

Description The large leaves grow in a thick clump straight from the ground, with white flowers on long sprawling stems. Once again it takes up rather a lot of space. It is said to need a rich, damp soil; frankly, it flourishes in any conditions.

Uses If you like exceptionally pungent horse-radish sauce, you may consider growing your own raw ingredients. The root is the part that is used. I am sometimes asked how a future supply of horse-radish can be ensured once the root has been dug up but this is not a problem. However hard you try to dig it all out there will always be a little piece left and the plant will spring up again and again as large as life. Think carefully before including it in your herb garden.

Sedum Acre and Sedum Album

Description Quite often seen in herb nursery catalogues, this creeping succulent with yellow-white flower heads will colonize an entire area before you can look round. Also known as 'biting stonecrop', it is a poisonous plant and thrives on dry shingly soil and is especially troublesome on gravel paths. Unless you can grow nothing else, avoid it.

Soapwort *Saponaria officinalis*

Description This relatively pretty pale pink flower – also known as 'bouncing Bet' – is very pushy. It has a creeping root-stock and spreads rapidly and is quite capable of ousting more submissive neighbours.

Uses The root makes a soapy solution which

Fig 35   Soapwort has pale pink flowers and grows in dry or difficult conditions, but it is inclined to be pushy.

Fig 36   Sedum acre, which has yellow flowers, and white-flowered Sedum album, colonize spare ground and gravel paths at an alarming rate.

has proved effective in cleaning old tapestries and delicate fabrics. It also makes a fairly ineffectual and unpleasant-smelling home shampoo. Soapwort is useful for difficult areas where other plants will not grow, as it tolerates the poorest of soils.

Tansy *Tanacetum vulgare*

Description   This is one to grow with caution. It is useful for covering a poor, dry area, near to a high moisture-stealing hedge, for example. Although invasive, it does not seed itself all over the place in the manner of the sedums above. The creeping roots can be contained in the same way as mint by putting in a brick or tile division. It has bright yellow button flowers in midsummer. There is also an attractive curled-leaf variety, *Tanacetum vulgare crispum.*

Uses   Despite what the books say, it is far too bitter to make a tansy pudding.

Yarrow *Achillea millefolium*

Description   There are various cultivated achilleas, and these are a different story. The medicinal herb, yarrow, is a rather tiresome roadside and garden weed. It has narrow, much-divided ground-hugging leaves from which emerge white flowers on 18in (45cm) stems. The tough, creeping roots are difficult to eradicate once they have a hold. This is a plant to avoid at all costs.

CHAPTER 2

Growing the Plants

The easiest way to get your herb garden established is to buy plants initially. However, there are some that it makes more sense to grow from seed. The chart on pages 46–7 suggests which herbs to buy – mainly the perennials – and which to grow from seed. It also indicates those which are easy to grow from cuttings, or runners, in case you are lucky enough to have a gardening friend with spare plant material.

BUYING HERBS

When buying herbs try to choose strong, healthy specimens. If a plant looks below par in the pot, it is no good thinking it will improve when planted out because it will not. The best guide is a common sense appraisal of the plant's appearance. If it looks straggly and thin with yellow or discoloured leaves, leave it on the staging. If, on the other hand, it has made plenty of bushy, fresh-coloured growth, it is probably healthy.

Check the apparent length of time it has spent in the pot. If the roots are struggling through at the bottom and the plant looks either stunted or

Fig 37   Always buy bushy, healthy-looking plants. It is a mistake to think that lank, sickly specimens will improve on planting out.

Fig 38   Roots struggling through at the bottom are a sure sign the plant has been too long in its pot.

Fig 39 *Tap the side of the pot to check if compost is loose. If in doubt, tip it out to check if roots are well developed.*

lank and overgrown, it is likely that it has been too long in its container. Some root showing is a good thing as it reveals a healthy well-developed root system. A gentle tug, or a tap on the side of the pot will indicate if the compost is loose and the plant has only just been potted up and has not had time to establish a strong root system. If in doubt, turn the pot on its side and tap the compost ball out (discreetly and without damaging the plant!) to check that the roots are well down. If the plant has been either too long or not long enough in its container, then do not buy it.

Plants often sell better when they are in flower but it is seldom a good idea to buy them at this stage as they will transplant more successfully if you catch them sooner. Buying an annual herb when it is in flower is a complete waste of money. It will not transplant and its life cycle is almost at an end.

Watch out for pests and diseases. Insects, such as red spider mite and whitefly, are very tiny and have a way of hiding on the under-sides of leaves. Avoid anything with wilting, discoloured or mouldy-looking leaves, which could be due to disease (See Chapter 7 on Pests and Diseases for further information.)

Some garden centres offer a reasonable range of herbs but specialist herb nurseries are preferable as they should know about their product and have the widest choice in the best condition. Herb nurseries are listed on pages 124–6. However, telephone numbers and addresses can change, so check with the British Herb Trade Association or the Herb Society, whose addresses are also on page 126, for up-to-date information.

Which Herbs to Buy and which to Grow from Seed

Those herbs that are easy to propagate by cuttings/division are marked either E = easy or VE = very easy.

Angelica   buy
Basil   seed
Bay   buy
Bergamot   buy
Borage   seed
Box   buy or cuttings (slow)
Bugle   buy or runners (VE)
Catmint   seed or buy
Camomile (Perennial)   buy or offsets (VE)
Camomile (Annual)   seed
Chervil   seed
Chives   buy or division (VE)
Coriander   seed
Costmary   buy or division (E)
Cotton Lavender   buy
Curry Plant   buy
Dill   seed
Elder (Ornamental)   buy

Elecampane   seed
Fennel   buy or seed
Feverfew   buy or seed
Good King Henry   buy or seed
Hyssop   buy or seed
Lady's Mantle   seed
Lavender   buy or cuttings (E)
Lemon Balm   buy or division (VE)
Lemon Verbena   buy
Lovage   buy
Marigold   seed
Marjoram   buy or division (E)
Annual marjoram   seed
Mint   buy or runners (VE)
Myrtle   buy
Nasturtium   seed
Orache   seed
Parsley   seed or buy
Pelargoniums   buy or cuttings (E)
Pennyroyal   buy or runners (E)
Pinks   buy or cuttings (E)
Rose   buy
Rosemary   buy or cuttings (E)
Rue   buy
Sage (Common)   buy or seed
Sage (Ornamental)   buy
Salad Burnet   buy or seed
Savory   seed
Sorrel   buy or seed
Southernwood   buy or cuttings (VE)
Sweet Cicely   buy
Tarragon   buy or division (E)
Thymes   buy or cuttings (E)
Wall Germander   buy, cuttings or division (VE)
Welsh Onion   buy, seed or division (E)
Wormwood   buy

PROPAGATING TECHNIQUES

Although you will start by buying plants, sooner or later you will want to increase or replace them. If you are planning an extensive scheme, it can work out very expensive to buy everything, so it is worth learning some simple propagating techniques. The main methods of propagating plants are by seed, by cuttings, or by division of the roots. Layering is also a useful technique.

Growing from Seed

As a general rule, do not waste money buying annuals potted up singly, grow them yourself from seed. You do not have to have a greenhouse to do this, although it will certainly help to get things off to a good start. The following herbs can easily be grown from seed:

Annuals   All are suitable; annual herbs include basil, borage, camomile (*Matricaria*), chervil, coriander, dill, pot marigold, nasturtium, red orache, summer savory, sweet marjoram.

Biennials   Angelica, clary sage, parsley (but treat this as an annual and sow fresh seed each year).

Perennials   Fennel, feverfew, hyssop, common sage, salad burnet, winter savory, lovage.

Sowing

Provided you wait until the soil has warmed up after the winter, seeds of hardy annual herbs can be sown directly into the ground where the plants are to grow. However, in many cases the success rate will be much higher if seeds are started off in seed-trays where they can be kept under controlled conditions.

Do not even consider sowing a tender plant like basil outside. It needs heat to germinate and heat for the young plants to develop. The half-hardy annual, sweet marjoram, is not as tender as basil, but it needs similar conditions. Parsley should always be sown in trays, to ensure success, as it needs heat to germinate. Herbs with very fine seed, like summer savory, are also best started in containers.

Water and heat are the two activators that induce a seed to come to life. In principle, the higher the heat – generally up to about 70°F (21°C) – the quicker the seed will germinate. In

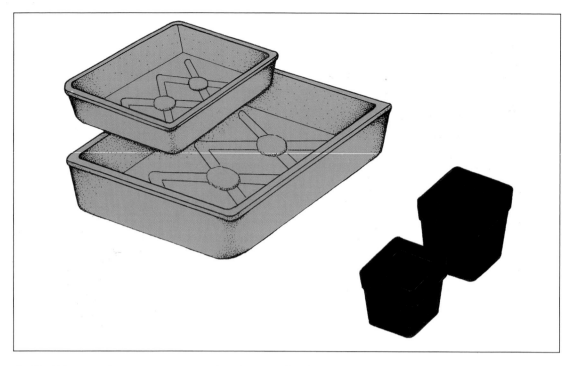

Fig 40 Full-size seed-trays present a mammoth pricking out task and provide too many seedlings for most gardens. Sow in half-size trays, or small pots. Square pots are best in a propagator.

practice, maintaining a sufficiently high and even temperature while the seedlings develop, and at the same time fulfilling their requirements for light and air, is not always easy for the home gardener. Compromises are necessary. This is why the timing of sowing is important.

Seed sown outside, straight into the ground, is especially vulnerable. If you start too soon, when it is cold and wet, the seeds may rot before they germinate. Once they do come through, there is a greater risk of set-backs. Young seedlings are liable to be checked by cold snaps, crushed by heavy rain-storms or hail and eaten by slugs and snails. It is usually best to wait until late April in temperate climates and May in cooler areas.

If you sow indoors or under glass too early, you have the problem of providing heat while seedlings develop. There is also the question of light. If seeds are started as early as February, light levels will be too low to sustain healthy growth (especially if seedlings have to be kept on a window-sill rather than in a greenhouse), and they will grow lank and weak.

The best compromise is to wait until artificial heat is only necessary for germination itself, after which seedlings can be kept in an unheated, frost-free greenhouse, or cold frame, before being hardened off outside ready for planting out. This will mean starting seeds at the end of March to mid-April in temperate climates (late April to beginning of May for tender plants like basil), and about three weeks later in colder areas, but be guided by each season's temperatures as well as by the calendar.

Seeds of hardy biennials (angelica and clary sage) should be sown in late summer in seed-trays, potted up and overwintered in a cold frame for planting out the following spring. However, you may never need to do this as they will seed themselves.

Seeds can be sown in trays or pots. Half-size trays will provide enough plants for most requirements and pots are useful if you only want a very few plants, and they will save space in a propagator. Full-size trays can be kept for pricking out. Herbs like dill, or coriander, which

Fig 41   Peat pots are useful for herbs, such as dill, which resent root disturbance.

resent root disturbance and have large seeds, can be grown in individual peat pots (as sometimes used for beans). These can then be planted out intact.

Hygiene is important in order to minimize the loss of seedlings through disease. Keep the work-bench, tools and all equipment clean and make sure that used seed trays are rinsed out and old, crusty tide-marks scrubbed off. Open bags or piles of discarded seed compost left lying about will harbour insects and the fungi responsible for damping-off disease. Clean out the greenhouse and ignite a pesticide smoke canister in it each year before starting your seeds to deter pests. (See Chapter 7 on Pests and Diseases.)

It is possible to mix your own seed compost but, unless you are raising plants on a large scale, it really is not worth the effort. Peat-based composts are easiest to use for seeds as they retain moisture best. There is no need to use a special 'seeds and cuttings' compost, an 'all-purpose' one is fine. With the call to cut down on the use of peat, you may prefer to use a John Innes compost, based on sterilized soil, but it is undoubtedly less satisfactory for the purpose of seed-raising.

Special requirements for individual herbs are given in Chapter 1. However, the basic process for sowing the seeds is the same for all:

Fill the container with compost to within ⅓in (1cm) from the top, filling it into the corners with the fingers and firming down gently with a presser (a board with a handle on top) to make an even surface. Seeds can be sown straight from the packet by tearing off a corner and tapping them out. But it is easier to get an even distribution by shaking some into one hand and then taking a few between the finger and thumb of the other hand, so that you can place them where you want them if they are large seeds, or scatter thinly if small. Make sure large seeds, such as borage, pot marigold, nasturtium and coriander, are spaced well apart so that there is no need for thinning out before transplanting. Do not forget to label the trays. Tiny seedlings of different plants can look very similar.

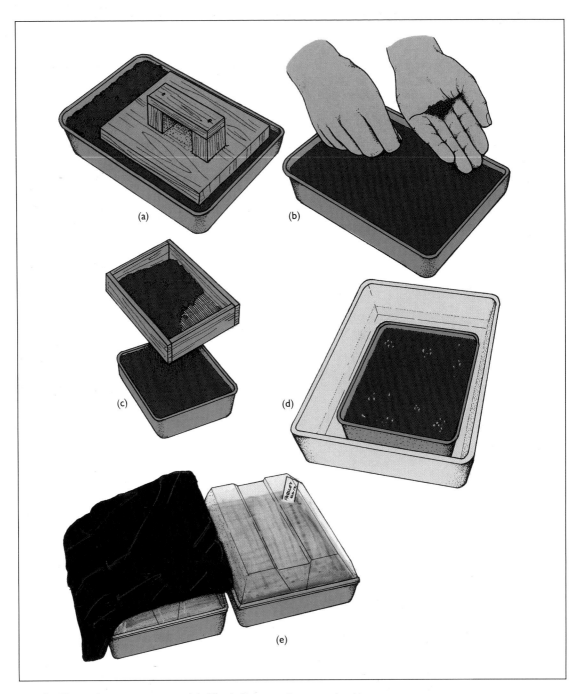

Fig 42 The seed sowing sequence: (a) Fill a half-size seed-tray evenly with an all-purpose peat-based compost. Use a presser board to achieve an even, but not compacted, surface. (b) Despite much received advice, sowing from the hand is much easier than tapping seeds out of a packet. (c) Cover seeds with a thin layer of sieved compost. (d) Stand the seed-tray in a pan of water until the surface of the compost glistens. (e) Enclose the tray in a polythene bag or purpose-made plastic seed-tray cover, and do not forget to label. Cover with black polythene, to exclude light, until seedlings first appear.

Sieve a very thin layer of compost over the top, ensuring that large seeds are completely covered but not too deeply. Water from underneath by standing the seed-tray in a large shallow container of water. This method avoids disturbing the placing of the seeds. You should cover the seed-tray with a plastic bag, or purpose-made plastic dome, to retain maximum moisture during germination. Lay black plastic or layers of newspaper over the top to exclude light and stand the tray where a temperature of 60–65°F (15–18°C) can be maintained.

Most herb seeds will germinate within days if a constant temperature of 68–70°F (20–21°C) is maintained. However, seedlings germinated at this temperature are liable to develop too quickly, becoming long and weak, before you manage to prick them out. They are also more inclined to break when being transplanted and are more vulnerable to disease, so a slightly lower temperature is preferable. An airing cup-

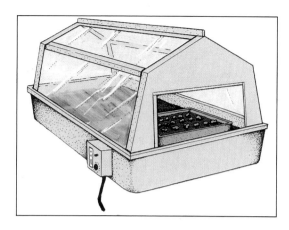

Fig 43   An electric propagating unit provides even heat and conserves moisture.

board is likely to be a little warmer than 70°F (21°C). An electric propagating unit that can be regulated to below 68°F (20°C) is ideal but a window-sill or shelf in a kitchen or utility room

Fig 44   Seed-trays enclosed in polythene bags on a window-sill are an effective way to start seeds.

can be just as effective and provide a suitable level of heat, although it may be necessary to ensure that night-time temperatures do not fall too low. An unheated greenhouse in March/early April will be too cold at night and often too hot on sunny days, unless well ventilated and shaded, so that germination will be erratic.

Keep a close watch on the seed trays and as soon as the first seed-leaves show through, remove the black covering and plastic bag or dome to give the developing plants air. If possible move them to a frost-free greenhouse, or conservatory, but make sure they get some shade as direct sunlight through glass will scorch them. If you leave them on a window-sill, the tiny plants will bend towards the light. Keep the seedlings well watered – but never too wet – using a fine rose and starting the spray to one side of the tray to avoid a deluge in one area.

As soon as the seedlings are large enough to handle, they should be either 'thinned' or 'pricked out' to give them room to grow. If they are left crowded together they will be starved of oxygen and unable to expand.

Fig 45   For an even spray that will not damage tiny seedlings, start watering to one side of the tray.

Thinning

Sometimes more seeds germinate than you will be able to use, in which case they can be thinned out in the tray, discarding the extra ones. This is a useful technique for basil which does not take kindly to root disturbance when the plants are small.

Pricking Out

For good-quality plants, try not to delay the pricking out process. Seedlings can be put in trays if many plants are required (such as a row of summer savory to plant around the beans). A full-size tray takes about thirty-five plantlets. Alternatively, they can be potted up individually in small pots. One seedling per pot will produce larger and stronger plants than those pricked out in trays.

Follow the stages below for pricking out:

1.   Fill another container, a tray or small pot, with fresh compost.
2.   Lift a clump of seedlings with a dibber. A strong plastic label is effective for this job.
3.   Separate one seedling, holding it by the leaves, so as not to damage the root. For seedlings like marjoram, which grow thickly together, separate into little clumps.
4.   Make a hole in the compost in the new container and replant the seedling, firming it in very gently to avoid crushing the roots.
5.   Water the seedlings carefully with a fine rose.
6.   Keep them in a frost-free greenhouse, or similar environment, until developed and large enough to plant out or pot on.

Potting On

Seedlings will need potting on before finding a final home if they have been thinned out in the tray. This will provide a better supply of food and prevent them from becoming thin and weak. It is likely that those that have already

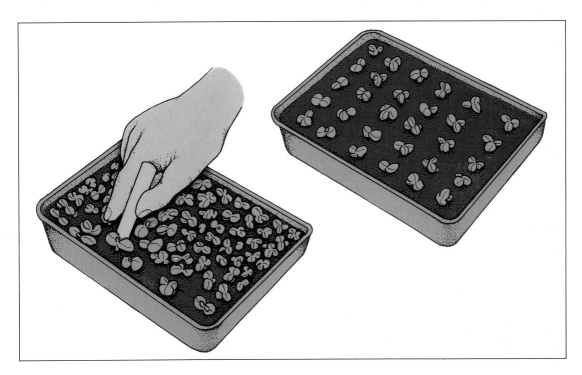

Fig 46   If there are more plants than you will need, and to minimize root disturbance at an early stage, thin basil seedlings out in the tray.

Fig 47   Pricking out seedlings. Seedlings need space to develop, so prick them out into trays as soon as possible. Seedlings pricked out in individual pots will make stronger plants.

Fig 48 (a) Well-rooted seedlings will need potting on. (b) Put a little compost in the pot. Hold the seedling in place and fill around the roots, being careful not to apply too much pressure, which will damage the roots. (c) Water in well.

been pricked out may need to be individually potted or, if originally pricked out into pots, moved to a pot a size larger, since this will help to produce more robust plants. It is not advisable to choose too large a pot as this encourages the compost to become sour and water-logged. Always go for the next size up.

It is difficult to make rules about potting on. It will depend on how long the seedlings are to be kept in small pots. Weather conditions, or time schedules, might make early planting out impossible, or you may want to grow some of your herbs on for fêtes or to give as presents.

Hardening Off

Up until this stage in their development, the plants have been cosseted. Therefore, it is important that they are hardened up for the rigours of outdoor life before being planted out. If you have a cold frame, you can transfer the trays, or pots, to this for a few days. If you do not have one, stand them outside in a sheltered place, bringing them in at night for a day or so, then leave them outside completely for a further few days before planting them in their final positions.

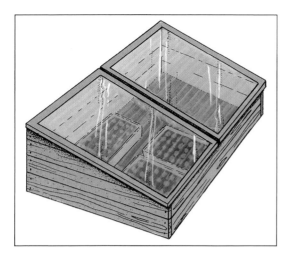

Fig 49 A cold frame is useful for hardening off young plants before putting them out in their final positions in the garden.

Growing from Seed without a Greenhouse

If you do not have a greenhouse, leave the sowing a week or two later, until outside temperatures are more settled. Germinate the seeds indoors, as previously described. Grow on the plantlets on a window-sill, turning daily to counteract bending to the light. Harden them off by standing the containers outside in a sheltered place and bringing them in at night for several days. Finally, leave them out completely for a further few days before planting out in the garden.

How to Succeed with Basil and Parsley

Of all the popular culinary herbs, the two which seem to present the most problems are basil and parsley. However, they are not really as difficult to raise and grow as they are popularly believed to be. It is only a question of understanding their needs and fulfilling their particular requirements. Follow the methods described below.

Basil If care is taken, you will have lovely bushy plants all summer long. Heat is the key. Basil is a tender plant, so delay sowing until mid to late April. If you start too early it will be much more difficult to provide suitable conditions for the developing plant. Sow the seeds thinly in seed-trays. With a constant temperature of 60–65°F (15–18°C) seeds will germinate within a week. If you do not have a heated propagator or greenhouse, keep the trays in a warm room. Once the seedlings are through, the trays can be moved to an unheated, but frost-free, greenhouse.

Basil is prone to damping-off disease, which makes the seedlings blacken and wilt. A close, over-humid atmosphere encourages this condition. To counteract it, provide adequate ventilation, plenty of light but not scorching sunlight, and keep the compost in the seed-trays moist but not too wet, and certainly not waterlogged.

Thin out seedlings in the tray as they begin to grow, and do not try to transplant them too soon. Once they have developed a stronger root system, the plantlets can be potted up, either individually in 3in (8cm) pots, or two to three in a 4in (10cm) pot. When they are strong and bushy, and all danger of frost is over – in late May or early June, according to where you live – pot them on into a larger container. Basil is much

Fig 50 Basil growing on in 4in (10cm) pots, after having been thinned out as seedlings.

Fig 51   Half-trays sown with flat-leaved and curly parsley. Heat is required for successful germination.

Parsley   Heat is also the key for parsley, but only for germination. It is slow to germinate compared with many herbs and in low temperatures often will not germinate at all. Forget all the advice about pouring boiling water over the seeds, just do not attempt to sow parsley directly into the ground. You can start sowing in March, if convenient, as parsley is not susceptible to frost, unlike basil. Sow it in seed-trays and keep these at a steady 65°F (18°C) until the seeds germinate, which will take a week to ten days. The seeds are very small, so beware burying too deeply. It is probably better not to cover with compost at all. Water from underneath after sowing (by standing the seed-tray in water) to avoid washing seeds away.

more successful when grown on in a large pot rather than planted out in the garden. Use a peat-based compost and water frequently. Pinch out the tips to encourage bushy growth.

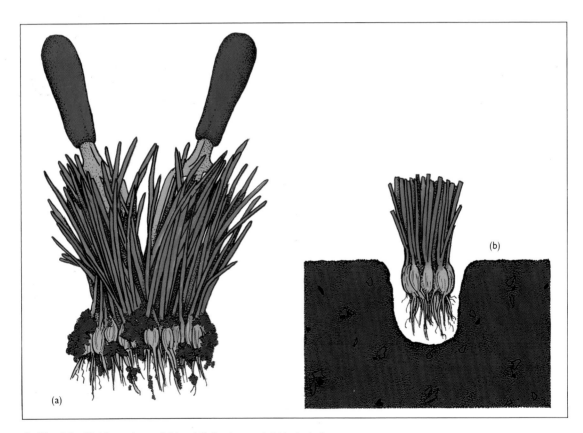

Fig 52   (a)   Dividing a clump of chives. Lift the plant and divide the bulbs, using two forks back-to-back, or pull apart with the hands if that seems easier.
(b)   Cut back the top growth by half and replant in a new position in the garden.

Once the seedlings are through, they will not need as much cosseting as basil. Transfer the trays to a cold greenhouse and the plants can be pricked out and transplanted to final positions in the usual way. Parsley does not resent being transplanted but it can be temperamental at the growing stage (remember, it is a biennial and will not go on for ever). However, if you grow it on in containers, in free-draining compost that you keep well watered, you should never have any trouble.

Vegetative Propagation

Increasing plants by division or by cuttings is known as vegetative propagation. This means that part of the growing plant is split off to form a new one. For some herbs it is the easiest method, although they can be grown from seed, and for others it is the only method, because they do not set seed, (French tarragon, for example) or do not breed true from seed (ornamental sages and thymes, for example).

Division of Roots

This is one of the easiest techniques as new plants are formed with ready-made roots. Herbs that can be propagated by division are:

Catmint, chives, marjoram, lady's mantle, lemon balm, bergamot, welsh onion and wall germander.

Spring or autumn is the time to do it. Generally, spring is preferable but on heavy or clay soils it is probably easier in autumn, before the ground gets clogged by winter rainfall. Dig up the plant you want to increase, or a part of it, remembering that the outside of the clump is usually the most vigorous part. Split it into sections with two forks, or by pulling it apart. Do not be afraid to deal firmly with it. Cut off the top growth to minimize loss of moisture, replant immediately and water thoroughly until it is established.

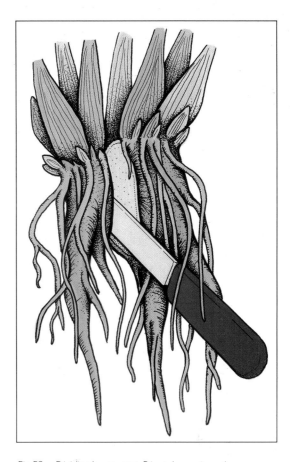

Fig 53   Dividing lovage root. Dig up lovage in early spring, before there is much top growth, slice the root into sections, ensuring that each piece has a bud. Replant each section so that it is just covered with soil.

Herbs with fleshy root tubers can also be propagated by dividing the roots. Lovage and sweet cicely, for example, can be increased in this way.

Offsets and Runners

This technique comes somewhere between division of roots and taking cuttings and it is suitable for plants which have creeping stems or which send out runners. The following herbs are suitable for propagating from offsets and runners:

Bugle, camomile (perennial), costmary, elecampane, mint, pennyroyal, tarragon and wormwood.

Camomile (*Anthemis nobilis* and 'Treneague')

This, most conveniently, produces new satellite plantlets, up to twenty per plant. These can be snipped off with secateurs, or a sharp knife, in early spring to form new plants. There is no need for a propagator or extra heat, they will root readily in pots in an unheated greenhouse or cold frame. Young camomile plants can be set out in their final positions as soon as they are sufficiently developed and will flower the same year.

Camomile plantlets can also be set straight into the open ground in April or May, but they will be at the mercy of the weather and less likely to root. To give camomile the best chance to root by this method, prepare the planting site well first, by digging in some compost and raking to an even tilth, then press each separated off-set into the ground, treading down firmly to encourage rooting. Space the new plantlets 9in–1ft (22–30cm) apart, if they are to be included in a border or general planting scheme. Water well and do not allow them to dry out until new roots have formed.

For a camomile lawn, path or seat, make sure you have the non-flowering 'Treneague' camo-

Fig 54   Propagating camomile from off-sets.   (a) Each camomile plant has up to twenty off-sets.   (b) In early spring, separate each plantlet, or 'off-set', with secateurs.   (c) Fill a 3in (8cm) pot with an all-purpose compost. Press the plantlet in well, water, and keep in a frost-free greenhouse, or cold frame until rooted.   (d) The new plants will be ready for putting out in the garden in just a few weeks.

Fig 55   Camomile can be planted among paving stones to make a scented path, but it will need plenty of maintenance.

mile. The plantlets should be spaced at 4–6in (10–15cm) intervals to form a close cover as quickly as possible. Hand weed regularly, especially during the first season, and keep well watered. Camomile can be walked on up to a point. It will not withstand heavy traffic and rough treatment and do give it a chance to become well established first.

Mint   This spreads by sending out runners and creeping underground stems. Take advantage of this characteristic to propagate it. Lift a runner, complete with underground stem, in early spring, as soon as you see the new growth start to show. Cut it in pieces at each joint where there is a shoot. The pieces should be about 1½in (4cm) long. Fill a container with a peat-based 'all-purpose' compost and plant each piece of stem in it, leaving the shoot to appear above the soil. Water in and keep the container

moist subsequently. Stand the container in a greenhouse or cold frame, shaded from direct sunlight. There is no need for artificial heat, but the warmer the conditions the quicker the cuttings will root.

Tarragon   This is another herb to propagate by means of its creeping underground stems. One way to do this is to lift a tarragon plant in the autumn. Cut back all the top growth and pot it up in a loam-based compost so that just the crown shows. Keep it in a frost-free, unheated greenhouse and, without letting it dry out completely, give it the minimum of water throughout the winter. In the spring, when the new roots start to come through, turn it out of the pot and divide the underground stems, so that each piece has a new shoot. Pot on separately and grow on until a new root system is formed. To increase tarragon that has been left in the ground

59

Fig 56   For new mint plants, lift a stem and divide it so that each piece has a
shoot.

Fig 57   (a) Tarragon's underground stems send out new shoots.   (b) Each
one makes a new plant.

through the winter, dig it up in March or April when the new shoots appear, divide the creeping roots and replant.

Cuttings

Taking cuttings from the stems in summer is the best way to propagate many herbs. Some respond to this technique more readily than others, two of the easiest being southernwood, *Artemisia abrotanum*, and pineapple sage, *Salvia rutilans*.

Plants vary as to the most suitable month for taking cuttings. Some can be taken with equal success throughout the summer but, in general, there are three periods to take stem cuttings, and three main categories of them:

1. Softwood cuttings are taken in spring and early summer from the new growth. These must be taken from herbs that root quickly (e.g. southernwood), as softwood cuttings do not have the capacity to survive for long without roots.

2. Semi-ripe cuttings are also taken from fresh growth but at a later stage when it is more mature. These cuttings can survive longer without roots and are the way to propagate herbs with a slow-rooting capacity (e.g. box). They are also used for herbs that should be overwintered under protection before planting out in spring (e.g. lavender). These cuttings are usually more successful if taken with a heel of old growth, from the main stem, attached.

3. Hardwood cuttings are taken when the plant is dormant and, apart from gallica and shrub roses, are not suitable for most herbs.

The table below indicates the best time for taking cuttings from individual herbs and how easily they root:

Pots are generally the most convenient containers for cuttings. They are easy to enclose in

Herbs to propagate from cuttings

	Most suitable time	Relative ease of process
Bay	August/September	Less easy
Box	August/September	Less easy
Cotton lavender	August/September or spring	Moderately easy
Curry plant	August/September	Moderately easy
Elder	May/June; Aug/September	Moderately easy
Hyssop	June/July	Moderately easy
Lavender	August/September	Moderately easy (expect some failure)
Lemon verbena	July/August	Less easy
Myrtle	September	Less easy
Pelargoniums	Through summer	Easy
Pineapple sage	Through summer	Very easy
Pinks	June/July	Easy
Rosemary	July/August	Moderately easy
Rue	June/July	Moderately easy
Sage (purple, tricolor icterina)	June/July	Less easy
Southernwood	May/June	Very easy
Thyme	Through summer	Moderately easy

polythene and, as cuttings nearest the edge of the container always seem to take best, round pots make the best use of space. A 5in (13cm) pot is a good size and will take five or six cuttings. For propagating plants that you are going to need in quantity, such as box or lavender for a hedge, a tray may be more convenient. The same rules of hygiene apply as for raising seedlings: make sure pots are scrubbed out and keep all equipment clean.

A mixture of sharp sand and peat, or a loam-based compost are the best media for most cuttings. The all-purpose peat-based seed and cuttings compost holds too much moisture for some plants, especially lavenders and thymes, and so encourages them to rot before they can root.

Warmth encourages roots to develop, and humidity is essential to keep cuttings alive until roots have formed to take on the task of providing the new plant with water and nutrients. To fulfil these conditions, there are several methods that can be used. The pot containing the cuttings can be enclosed in a polythene bag. Care must be taken not to let the polythene collapse onto the cuttings, as this could suffocate and drench them. Shrubby herbs with needle-like leaves, such as rosemary and thyme, also lavender and other silver-leaved herbs, need less humidity and do better if not enclosed in polythene. An inexpensive propagating unit with a plastic dome but no heating element is an effective way to start many cuttings, but make sure you choose one that has ventilation. A heated propagation unit is the next stage up. Bottom heat encourages root development. Another

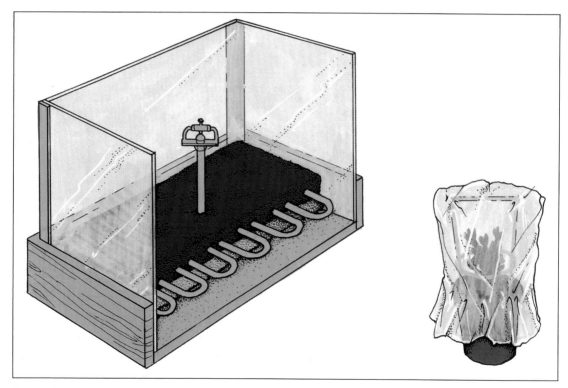

Fig 58   A mist propagation unit provides ideal conditions for most cuttings. A polythene bag, supported by sticks or a frame, over a pot, maintains a humid atmosphere and is a simple alternative which suits some plants very well.

Fig 59 (a) Southernwood (Artemisia abrotanum) cuttings root very quickly if taken in early summer. Cut off a stem from the new sappy growth (hard pruning in autumn will ensure vigorous spring growth). (b) Cut the stem into 3in (8cm) pieces at the leaf joints. (c) Prepare the cutting by snipping away lower leaves.

method is a mist propagator, which is ideal for most cuttings. It keeps them moist automatically and provides bottom heat. As it is an open unit, the surrounding air does not become too damp or too hot, both of which are counter-productive for many shrubby herbs and can occur with the polythene bag method. However, this equipment is expensive and not always necessary for the home gardener, although it is useful for some of the herbs that are trickier to propagate, such as lemon ver-bena. It all depends how ambitious you want to be with the amount and variety of cuttings you attempt. For most purposes, the first or second methods are more than adequate.

You should consult the table for the optimum month or months for taking cuttings from the parent plant of a particular herb. Softwood cuttings taken from the new season's growth should be severed below a leaf joint at a node. Cuttings taken later in summer can be made a little lower, between leaf joints. Some plants, such as lavender, take better from heel cuttings, i.e. new side-shoots are stripped away with a piece of heel from the old stem still attached. Cuttings from flowering herbs, such as thyme, should be taken from non-flowering shoots.

Do not take too many cuttings at once and risk them wilting before they can be dealt with. Enclose them in a polythene bag if there is likely

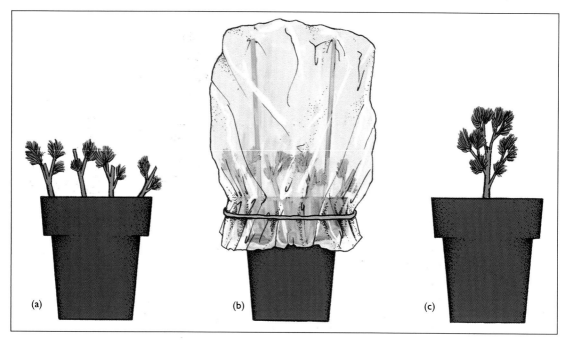

Fig 60 *(a) Set the southernwood cuttings around the edges of a pot.*
(b) Enclose the pot in polythene as shown. (c) Once the cuttings have made
new growth, pot them up separately.

Fig 61 *Lavender cuttings are taken later in*
summer and root more readily if a small heel of the
old stem is left attached. This is achieved by
stripping off the side-shoots with the fingers.

to be a short delay. The cuttings should be prepared by snipping off all but two or three leaves. Dip the base of each prepared cutting into hormone powder, tapping off any excess. Then, fill a pot with a suitable cuttings medium and make holes with a dibber round the edge. Put a cutting into each hole and fill in lightly. A cutting in the central position is less likely to take.

For softwood cuttings, and quick-rooting herbs, enclose the pot in a polythene bag held away from the cuttings by four sticks or a simple frame. For most semi-ripe cuttings and shrubby herbs, which dislike too much moisture (e.g. lavender, rosemary, thyme), do not use the polythene bag method. Stand them in a shady place, on a window-sill or in a greenhouse, until rooted. Slow-rooting herbs can be put in a cold frame or frost-free greenhouse.

Cuttings will develop roots within anything from a few weeks to several months. When there are signs of adequate new growth, pot each cutting up separately. Do not put newly rooted young plants straight into pots that are much too large for them, to save on re-potting,

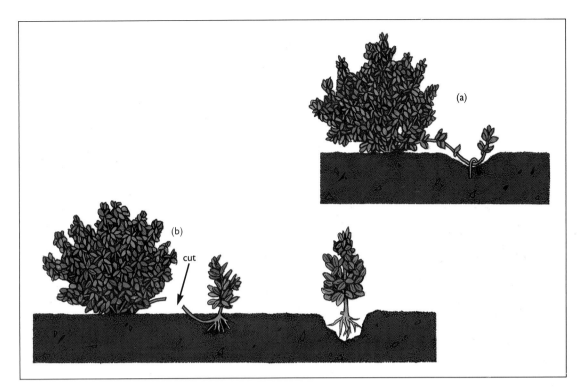

Fig 62 (a) Sage can be increased by the technique of 'layering'. In the spring, bend over a side-shoot and bury the stem in well-prepared soil, fixing it with a staple and leaving the growing tip showing. (b) In the autumn, if the layered stem has rooted (in the following spring if it has not), cut the connecting branch, dig up the new plant and re-position where required.

as the compost will become wet and stale and the plants will not develop properly.

Some quick-developing cuttings taken early in the year, such as southernwood, can be planted out as soon as they are sufficiently developed. Others can be planted out in the autumn or kept through the winter in a cold frame or an unheated but frost-free, greenhouse, and planted in the spring. A few slow-growing herbs, such as bay and box, should be kept for two seasons before the final outside planting. These should be potted on, using fresh compost, in the second year, to provide the growing plant with nutrients. Plants which are not always reliably hardy, such as rosemary, should be given some protection the first winter they are planted out.

Layering

This is a method of propagating new plants while they are still attached to the parent. Herbs to increase by layering are:

Cotton lavender, curry plant, pinks, rosemary, and sage, which is one of the most suitable herbs for this method. Thymes will often self-layer.

Cultivate the soil around the plant by digging in compost and grit in spring. Choose a low-growing side-stem, and trim off the lower leaves if necessary. Dig a shallow channel where the chosen stem will touch the ground. Bend it over, burying part of it, and fasten it down in the soil with a staple. Water it well, and by autumn the layered stem should have made new roots. (If these do not seem to have developed adequately, leave it until the following spring.) Sever the newly layered plant from its parent and replant in a new position in the garden or in a container.

CHAPTER 3

Designing the Herb Garden

FIRST CONSIDERATIONS

Having spent a little time familiarizing yourself with the plants, visiting other people's herb gardens, making notes and taking photographs, you can start to plan your own scheme. You will, of course, be guided by your own preferences and requirements, but it will be helpful to take the following considerations into account:

Think about your main reason for growing herbs, whether it is to provide fresh herbs for the kitchen, to provide material for pot-pourris and scented preparations, to make herb teas

Fig 63   A newly planted knot garden, no more than 12 sq ft (3.6 sq m) square.

Fig 64 *A small fountain garden planted with fragrant herbs and bordered by a trellis, supporting a climbing rose (Hollington Nurseries).*

and home remedies, or simply because you are drawn to herbs because of their romantic associations and the image they project of fragrant, sunny days in a calmer, less frantic age. Your motives are more than likely a mixture of the practical and the romantic, but if you can identify an area of interest it will help you to get started.

The size of your garden, or the amount of space available for herbs, will to a certain extent dictate your design. However, even in a very small garden there are endless possibilities. A herb border or island bed of herbs can be fitted into any existing garden scheme, and a cartwheel or ladder shape takes up little space. A self-contained rectangular plot of 10 × 12ft (3 × 3.6m) gives plenty of scope for an all-purpose or culinary herb garden, a small theme garden or a formal or knot garden. And do not forget that

herbs can be grown throughout the garden, you do not need to consign them to a special area. Many provide fragrance and interest in a mixed border, some make sympathetic bedfellows for roses and others are a must in the vegetable plot. One of the best ways of growing herbs for the kitchen is to have a collection of pots on the patio.

It might seem obvious, but do take into account the amount of time you can spend on your herb garden. Knot gardens, for instance, take a great deal of maintenance. To be successful they need to be kept manicured, which means frequent and accurate clipping and trimming. It is so easy to be inspired by beautiful illustrations in old books but remember that many traditional gardens were very labour intensive. Even apparently informal plantings can take a lot of work, and few of us – I imagine – are in the happy position of someone like Gertrude Jekyll, who designed her borders with an artist's eye and the help of many gardeners. It will certainly pay dividends to think about the maintenance when working out the design.

CHOOSING THE SITE

Many herbs come from the Mediterranean region and flourish in warm sun and light soil. This should be taken into account when choosing the site for a herb garden. Look for a south, or south-west facing aspect and make sure the area will not be covered by dense shade for too much of the day.

See that the site is sheltered from strong prevailing winds, a north-easterly is especially hard for herbs to bear. Consider how you could improve matters, if necessary, with walls, fencing or hedges. An example of this can be seen at Harlow Car Gardens, near Harrogate, where the herb garden is intended primarily as a hedging and ground cover demonstration garden. Rosemary, lavender and purple sage, all of which can take offence to cold winds and low temperatures, grow successfully there within the shelter of the hedges. It is worth remembering that early monastery gardens (which were to a great extent responsible for establishing herb growing in Britain) provided an ideal microclimate, being sited within the shelter of the cloisters.

A light, free-draining soil is best for most herbs. If you do have to garden on heavy clay, it can always be improved by digging in plenty of grit or a mixture of perlite and peat. However, many herbs, such as lavender and thyme, will never flourish in a clay soil. If, at the other extreme, your soil is very gravelly and dries out too quickly, it will pay to dig in plenty of well-rotted compost or manure to improve the soil structure. As a general rule, herbs grow better if slightly 'stressed' rather than pampered. They do not need a rich soil, which will only promote weakening, lush growth at the expense of maximum scent and flavour.

Herbs can be untidy in growth and the discipline imposed by formal patterns compensates for this tendency. For the same reason, geometric-shaped beds show the plants off to advantage. In the more informal style of design, there is a place for curves and flowing edges, but even informal herb gardens, beds or borders are improved by having a definite structure.

STRUCTURE

The structure of the garden will be provided by its edging and general outline, by the paths and divisions within it and further defined by features and focal points. It may be helpful to think of the structure as the 'skeleton', which will be fleshed out and given body, form and features by the plants. After all, a body without a skeleton would collapse into an amorphous mass.

Paths and Divisions

Apart from providing structure, paths make it possible to get close to the plants to pick, smell and enjoy them. In the smallest bed, there is a place for stepping-stones placed amongst the herbs (perhaps placed in a random pattern), and in most areas that are over 5 or 6sq ft (0.5–0.6 sq m) paths or divisions are essential.

Old brick is a sympathetic material to use for herb garden paths. The minimum width for a path in a small area garden would be of three bricks, with the central one laid lengthways and the outer ones at right-angles to it. This kind of path is very easy to lay and lasts well if you use hard, impermeable, frost-resistant bricks. A hard-core base is not necessary, provided the ground is level and well-compacted.

Shingle is relatively cheap and easy to lay. The colours available and texture make it a good foil for herbs. Lay it over heavy-duty polythene to prevent weeds coming through. An edging of brick, tiles or wood is recommended to prevent

Fig 65 An old brick path.

Fig 66 A natural stone path.

it from spreading onto beds. The depth to lay shingle varies according to use, but at least ½in (1cm) depth is needed, and 1in (2.5cm) is really preferable.

Natural stone, either in slabs or as crazy-paving looks good. Making sure the base is firm and level, lay the stone on a layer of sand or, for a more permanent structure that will discourage weeds, bed it into mortar or concrete. Cobbles make a most attractive finish, and are ideal for small areas. Pack them together as closely as possible, either setting them into concrete on a hard-core base, or putting them on a dry mortar or concrete base and watering in with the hose.

You should consider carefully before choosing either modern paving slabs or grass for paths. The former can look out of place, unless used with discretion, perhaps in conjunction with more traditional materials, and the latter look very attractive but create work as they have to be kept mown and edged. Grass paths can also get rather worn-looking in a dry summer if much walked on so a hard surface is generally preferable.

Large beds and borders will look better and be more manageable if they are laid with bricks,

Fig 67 A grass pathway.

or if tiles are pushed into the soil, in order to divide the area into smaller units. This technique also has the effect of preventing invasive herbs, such as mint, from encroaching on neighbours.

Focal Points and Features

A focal point, usually in the centre of the garden, gives it form. A fountain or a sun-dial are traditional central features. A standard bay or box, or a raised urn containing an eye-catching plant – trailing nasturtiums, perhaps – also make arresting centre-pieces. Alternatively, you could find a place for an old-fashioned 'bee-skep', which is a dome-shaped hive made of thick woven straw, and was popular in early American 'colonial' gardens. Unusual statuary, old chimney pots, or any large and interesting con-

tainers, such as an 'Ali Baba' jar, will add impact to an odd corner.

A tranquil place where you can sit and enjoy the scents and sights of the garden is a must. There are a multitude of garden chairs and benches on the market; your choice will depend on your taste and your pocket. A sheltering arbour over the seat, or an archway covered with a scented climber, make it a pleasant place to linger. A tall hedging plant, such as hawthorn, could also be trained to form an arbour.

Camomile seats were popular in Tudor gardens and make a most appealing feature. The easiest way to construct one is by making use of an existing steep bank or raised bed. Build a low retaining wall to form the front of the seat, edging the top with bricks or timber to form a container which can then be planted with

Fig 68   These charming stone figures welcome visitors to the potager garden at Barnsley House.

Fig 69   Camomile seats were a feature of Tudor gardens. Clipped box forms the back-rest and arms.

camomile. Use the non-flowering 'Treneague' camomile (which is also best for lawns), and set the plants about 6in (15cm) apart. Keep the seat well-weeded and watered, clipping annually in early summer. The back and arms of the seat can be made of brick, or it would be more traditional to use clipped box.

Height is important to create interest. Old-fashioned roses, grown as standards, are useful here, as are pyramids of box or bay. Standards can be sited symmetrically around a central diamond or circle, or placed at strategic intervals in a bed or border. There are many climbing plants that can be grown over twiggy bowers, or as wigwams. Sweet peas, honeysuckle and hops are three that are especially suited to the herb garden. A wrought-iron or metal-framed gazebo, supporting scented plants, such as climbing roses or jasmine, are a more perma-

nent way of introducing height to the scheme, and if you are lucky enough to have a stone pavilion or summer-house of a suitably sympathetic construction, this could be made central to your overall design.

Enclosures

The most interesting herb gardens have a definite boundary which separates them from their surroundings. An enclosing hedge, wall or trellis fence, with an opening or archway that invites you to walk in, creates the illusion of a secret, self-contained world. This is much more beguiling than having everything laid out at your feet, visible at first glance.

A tall, dense hedge, such as yew, makes a good back-drop for a herb garden. However, as it will take some years to achieve a height of 7ft

(2m), it is not the one to choose for instant results, unless, of course, you have inherited a ready-made yew hedge in just the right place. For a quicker-growing hedge, consider a row of ornamental elders (tall), or a rose hedge such as a sweet briar, or *Rosa rugosa* (medium, 4–5ft/1.2–1.5m). Hawthorn, with its lovely May blossom, is another quick-growing traditional herb garden hedge. Espaliered fruit trees also make an effective screen.

For herb gardens that are too small to be enclosed by walls or high hedging, the lower-growing herbal hedging plants provide appropriate boundaries. Dwarf box is the favourite for this purpose and is ideal for creating a formal look but, unless you raise all your own plants, it can be rather expensive. Young box plants need to be placed about 6in (15cm) apart to form a close hedge. (*See* Chapter 1 on Plant Profiles, and Knot Gardens in Chapter 1 for more detailed advice on box).

Wall germander, with its glossy dark green leaves makes an attractive low hedge. It should be planted at 9in (22cm) intervals and kept low and tidy by cutting back before the purply flowers appear in late summer. Hyssop can also be used as a low hedge plant but, as its blue flower spikes are its chief attraction, it is a pity to have to cut it back to keep it in a neat hedge-shape. It is more suitable for a lax, informal edging which is allowed to flower.

Lavender and rosemary, which are both highly fragrant, make lovely hedges, especially if planted against a low wall. Cut rosemary back lightly in the spring, after flowering, to maintain tidy growth and prevent it growing too tall. Lavender provides plenty of choice; there is the low-growing 'Munstead' and 'Hidcote' and many taller varieties also. In all cases, keep lavender well trimmed to prevent it becoming straggly. Do not be afraid to cut it back hard as soon as it has flowered in late summer.

Herb beds and boundaries can be edged with clipped mounds of plants such as rue, golden marjoram or cotton lavender (*Santolina*). These can be planted about 1ft (30cm) apart and kept

Fig 70 *An arbour of hawthorn and honeysuckle over a seat was a feature of many 16th and 17th century gardens.*

regularly trimmed to maintain the dome shape. Chives are a trouble-free edging as they need little maintenance. The purple flower-globes are strikingly ornamental.

Trellis-work makes a romantic enclosing framework and has the added advantage of providing support for scented climbers. However, it does need to be very firmly grounded and is likely to have a more limited life than walls or hedging. Red cedarwood is the

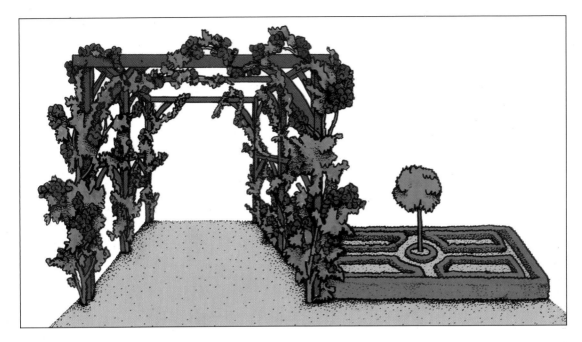

Fig 71   An arbour, or 'herber', also meant a covered walk. In Tudor gardens, these were made from sections of shaped timber, over which climbing plants were trained.

most long-lasting, but also the most expensive. A low paling fence can look just right and, for a small garden, a simple post and rail construction at each corner provides an illusion of an enclosure.

In the sixteenth century, the 'herber' or 'arbour' was either a place to sit or, very often, a covered walkway with climbing plants growing over a wooden arched framework. If you have the time and the financial resources for something elaborate, an arbour walk, clothed in jasmine, roses or other scented climbers would make a romantic 'boundary' for the larger herb garden.

Another idea which can be adapted for the modern herb garden, is the 'apple-walk' (of course, this could be substituted with another fruit-tree) of the medieval monastery. To construct an apple-walk, you should start by erecting a tunnel of connected archways, made of tubular steel wtih black nylon coating. (Various

firms sell ready-to-assemble systems). A span of 5ft (1.5m) and a height of 6ft 6in (2m) is a good measurement to work from. The length will depend on your particular plot. Plant two-year-old cordon-pruned fruit trees at the base of each arch, on both sides, attaching the single stem to an upright, and the lateral, fruit-bearing side-spurs to the side-struts. Keep tying the branches in as they grow to keep the shape. It will take about six years for the leading shoots to meet at the apex of the arch (when they can be pruned, or grafted together) and for a thick tunnel of growth to form.

Old brick walls always make an excellent back-drop to the herb garden. They do not have to surround it completely. One possibility would be to have a wall flanking just one side, with a line of espaliered fruit trees forming another side and low herbal hedging plants, such as lavender or rosemary, forming the remaining sides.

Raised beds with timber or brick edgings are

73

Fig 72 An apple-walk. Cordon-pruned apple trees, trained over a series of archways, will eventually form a thick tunnel of foliage. This is a method of growing fruit which dates back to medieval times.

another way to give form to the herb garden and make the area stand out from the surroundings. They can also be an advantage where the soil is heavy and unsuitable for growing herbs, as raised beds are freer-draining and can be filled with a growing medium that they will find compatible.

HERB BEDS AND BORDERS

The simplest way to start a herb garden is to allocate a bed or border for the purpose. Either make use of an existing one or dig out a new shape. For the outline, simple geometric shapes are easy to construct and can look very effective.

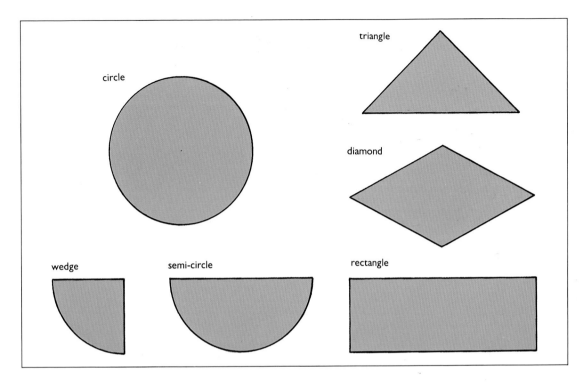

circle

diamond

wedge   semi-circle   rectangle

Fig 73   Herb beds and borders based on geometric shapes are easy to lay out.

Geometric Shapes

A 'herb wheel', filled with plants chosen for their contrasting colours and textures, makes an imaginative feature. For maximum impact, keep it simple and do not go for too many divisions. If you use a cartwheel, the spokes will be too close together for sensible planting so it will be best to remove some. Treat the wheel with wood preservative before laying it on a circular bed. It will probably be easiest to support it in the middle and at two or three places round the circumference on bricks, using a spirit level to check that it is lying evenly. Make sure the spaces between the spokes are well filled with soil before planting. A herb wheel can also be constructed from brick in the form of a raised bed. A circle 6ft (1.8m) in diameter, with six divisions, and sides two bricks deep, is a good model to work from.

A semi-circular bed can be fitted into the smallest garden. With a straight side, 9ft (2.7m) long and 4½ft (1.3m) across at the widest point,

it can be planted to provide a good selection of herbs for the kitchen.

A narrow border by the back door could be transformed into a 'ladder of herbs'. Mark out a 12ft (3.6m) border and divide it into six 2ft (60cm) square plots, using brick divisions or roofing tiles set sideways into the soil. (This will prevent invasive herbs spreading into each

Fig 74   The herb wheel at The Herb Farm, Sonning Common, contains, from left to right, Stachys lanata (lamb's ears) at centre back, pot marigold, camomile, Santolina viridis, rue and purple sage.

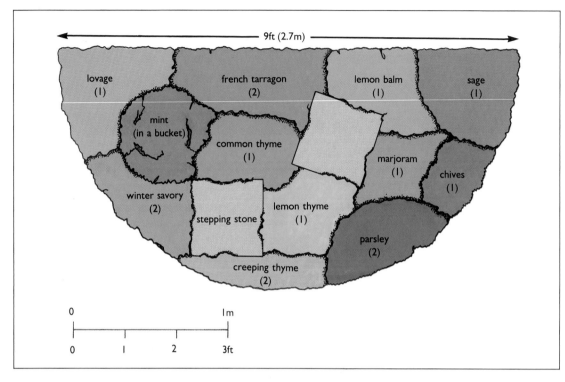

Fig 75   Plan for a semi-circular kitchen garden. With one each of the larger herbs and two of some of the others, this compact garden will provide a good supply of popular culinary herbs.

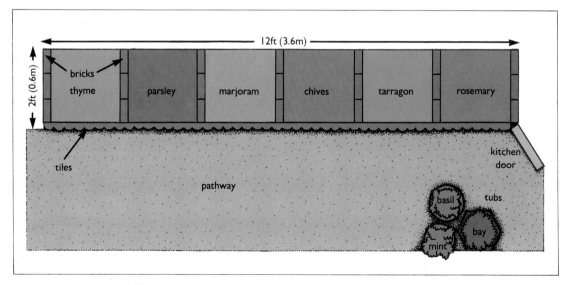

Fig 76   A plan for a ladder of herbs.

other.) Keep each compartment for a separate herb. To complete the scheme, herbs such as basil and bay, can be grown in tubs near the back door.

The wedge is a most useful shape which will fit into many existing garden schemes. The wall of the house might form one of the straight edges, thus providing protection from cold winds and a support for climbing plants, with the other straight edge facing on to a pathway. If the straight sides are 7–8ft (2.1–2.4m), this will make quite a large bed which can be planted with a good mixture of herbs. Stepping stones should be placed among the plants for ease of access.

A diamond shape would be ideal for an island bed of fragrant and aromatic herbs. Plant something moderately tall in the centre, such as a shrub rose, surround it with catmint and edge with a creeping ground cover, such as bugle (*Ajuga reptans*) – the purple or the multi-coloured variety would look best. If the bed is not large, do not try to put too many different herbs in. Plants of one kind, massed together, nearly always make more impact.

Irregular Shapes

Although formal geometric shapes are both traditional and satisfying to the eye in a herb garden, there is a place for more flowing lines as well.

An irregular semi-circular shape, planted with several varieties of creeping thyme to form a 'thyme river', is easy to look after and creates a colourful corner. Laid out as a raised bed, edged

Fig 77   A 'river of thyme', complete with wooden bridge, makes the most of different levels of ground (The Herb Farm, Sonning Common).

with timber or brick, it will provide the free-draining conditions in which thymes flourish. Make sure the bed is weed-free and put the plants in 6in (15cm) apart. To achieve a flowing 'river' effect, the plants should not be set in straight rows and the different varieties should be planted to blend into each other. Any of the low-growing creeping thymes would be suitable. Choose a selection that has varying flowering periods and colours. Hand weed carefully until they have grown together to form a dense cover and keep well-trimmed, cutting back hard after flowering, so that a neat finish is maintained.

Larger Borders

Larger borders (shrub or herbaceous borders that have passed their prime) can be trans-

formed into self-contained herb gardens. Start by putting in some divisions of single brick, or tiles laid on edge. Narrow pathways can also be incorporated. The latter need not be more than two bricks wide as their purpose is to break up the area and provide access, rather than to act as proper paths. When planning the planting, do not forget to put taller plants at the back. In a long, narrow border, an interesting effect can be achieved by placing tall herbs at intervals down the length with lower-growing ones in between.

A most interesting informal herb border has been planted at Jesus College, Cambridge, to replace an old shrubbery. Circular terracotta tile 'pockets' echo the curved outlines of the border, and stepping stones in a contrasting light-grey give access to the centre. Wooden tubs, planted with fragrant lemon verbena and herbs with

Fig 78   In this wide border, semi-circular narrow brick paths have been put in to give access to the plants.

Fig 79 and 80   The herb garden at Jesus College, Cambridge, shows how a
mature effect can be achieved quickly by planting with herbs. There is just three
months between these pictures from planting in mid-March (above) to full bloom
in mid-June (below).

colourful flowers, such as blue flax and bright yellow dyers' camomile, have been cleverly sited to hide old drain covers. Head gardener, Paul Stearn, who designed the garden, decided to keep the planting simple for maximum impact and chose four main species – bergamot, sage, mint and thyme – to provide colour and interest over a long period. The thymes and mints are kept in check by the tile pockets.

TRADITIONAL SCHEMES FOR LARGER HERB GARDENS

In this section, some different approaches to planning a complete herb garden scheme are suggested, with plenty of examples of successful, existing gardens to provide ideas and inspiration. Not all the suggested outline designs are given with complete planting schemes. This is in order to give scope for individual preferences and situations. But it is impossible to separate layout and purpose completely, so general ideas for appropriate planting are proposed.

In the earliest gardens, two basic structures for the overall layout predominated. These have influenced herb garden design ever since. The first is a grid pattern, made up of a number of rectangular beds arranged in regular rows. It has been suggested that this layout has its origins in early Persian gardens, which were constructed in this way for ease of irrigation. Many formal Renaissance gardens followed this general scheme, as can be seen from paintings and plans of the period, but the designs within each element of the grid had become, in many cases, very complex.

The second basic pattern is that of a cruciform shape, which was inspired by the Christian tradition and formed the structure of many early monastery gardens. Very often the two were combined, the overall layout being in a grid pattern, with the central path forming a pronounced cross, and the cross being echoed in each square, making up the grid.

A Cruciform Garden

The cruciform layout is extremely versatile and provides a good starting point for designing an all-purpose herb garden of manageable proportions, which will fit into the framework of an average-sized existing garden. An overall size of approximately 20 × 15ft (6 × 4.5m) would allow plenty of space for a varied selection of culinary and ornamental herbs.

The herb garden at the American Museum, Claverton Manor, near Bath, is a variation on the cruciform theme. Only half the cross is complete, so it forms one large encircling bed and one balancing smaller, single bed. It is a compact garden, being about 21 × 16ft (6.3 × 4.8m) and would fit well into a smaller, more domestic setting. Surrounded by dwarf box hedging, the beds are filled with a variety of aromatic, culinary and medicinal plants. A traditional woven straw bee-skep forms the focal point. The same stone paving-slabs that make up the adjoining terrace continue into the herb garden, with a double row of cobblestones delineating the boundary of the garden.

A much larger herb garden following the basic cruciform pattern can be seen at Hatfield House, Hertfordshire. It is about 30 × 50ft (9 × 15m) and is enclosed by hedges of sweet briar (mainly *Rosa rubiginosa*). It is a garden within a garden, being set within a larger walled area, known as 'The Sweet' or Scented Garden. The central path of the herb garden is bordered with lavender, and the cross converges at a handsome sundial set in the focal point. Camomile is planted around the base of the sundial and in the centre of the paving slabs at the entrance to the garden. Honeysuckles, trained as standards, are planted around the central circular area, with dramatic red orache and golden sage complementing the misty-blue of the lavender and providing colour after the roses have finished blooming.

The many old-fashioned roses are a feature of the garden and include the *gallica* roses, 'Rosa Mundi', 'Belle Isis', and 'Tuscany Superb'; the

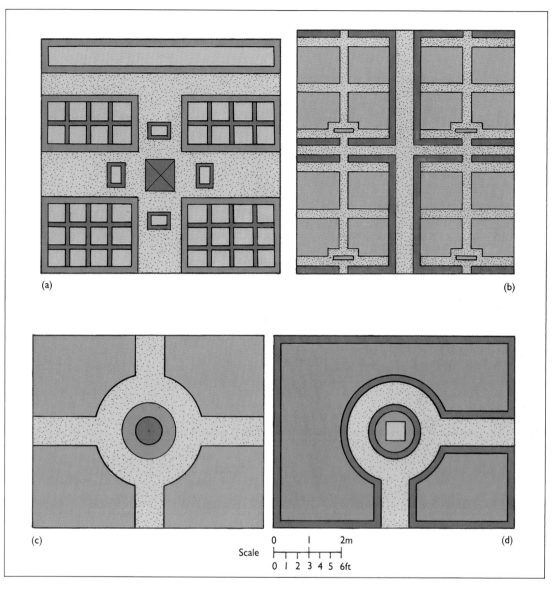

(a)   (b)

(c)   (d)

Scale

0   I   2m

0 I 2 3 4 5 6ft

Fig 81 (a) Whilst the basic grid shape was retained, the cross became a
dominant motif in Renaissance gardens. (b) Early Eastern gardens were laid out
in a grid pattern for ease of irrigation. (c) An outline for a traditional herb garden.
(d) A plan of the herb garden at the American Museum, Claverton Manor, Bath.

damask roses (R. damascena) 'Celsiana' and
'Painted Damask', and the old cabbage rose,
R. centifolia. These are planted amongst a wide
range of traditional herbs, such as rue, rosemary,
mint, coriander, sage, tansy, hyssop, southernwood, lemon balm and thyme. Laced pinks
provide an authentic romantic touch and tulips,
iris and primulas are included for spring interest.

Taller herbs, lovage and green and bronze
fennel, are planted at the outer corners.

Garden Based on Geometric Shapes

A straightforward way to design a complete
garden is to follow the Renaissance style in a

scaled-down, simplified version. This can be done by building on the basic geometric-shaped single bed (circle, triangle, rectangle or square), repeating it to form a regular pattern.

A garden of four wedge-shaped beds at the outer corners, with a central circular bed is easy to lay out. This pattern lends itself to a scented garden. Paths could be of paving or grass, with the beds edged in box, chives or wall germander. Features such as a gazebo to support climbing scented plants, or a fountain in the central bed, could be added in time.

The same principle can be followed using the triangle as a template to make a garden with a diamond-shaped central bed surrounded by four triangular beds. A herring-bone pattern brick path would suit this design, with a sundial as a central feature. To avoid a bitty look, keep to the same plant for edging the four smaller beds and plant tall herbs at the outside corners. Ornamental herbs can be grown in the central bed, silvery-leaved plants such as curry and cotton lavender, perhaps, with pinks and a central standard bay tree or clipped ornamental box. In the four outer beds a selection of culinary and medicinal herbs could be planted.

Rectangular-shaped beds can be laid out in many different combinations to form pleasing patterns. Each bed can be devoted to a single herb (a traditional way of planting often seen in old manuscript illustrations), or planting can be more varied, depending on the size of the beds. Rectangles are highly suitable for raised beds. They also make a good design for a garden of culinary herbs.

A repeated 'cartwheel' motif has been used very successfully in the herb garden at Stockeld Park, North Yorkshire. In an area approximately 30ft (9m) square, four large circular beds, 10ft (3m) in diameter, surround four smaller circular beds, with a sundial at the central focal point. The surrounds of the beds are of concrete, set into gravel, and the outer beds have concrete divisions forming the spokes. The centres of these larger beds are planted with cupressus 'Sky-rocket', which gives the scheme height.

Fig 82   In the herb garden at Hatfield House, rare old-fashioned roses are planted in profusion along with lavender, sage and a wide variety of culinary and aromatic plants.

. When planting up a cartwheel design such as this, care must be taken not to unbalance the design. Put the tallest plants in the centres and on the inward-facing segments of the outer circles. Plant smaller herbs in the inner circles. These smaller beds can also be appropriately planted with a single variety, such as mint.

THEME GARDENS

If you find it confusing, when planning the planting, to include herbs across the whole range available, try grouping them by themes. A whole garden can be devoted to a theme, or separate beds within a larger garden can each take a subject of their own. Culinary herbs and the

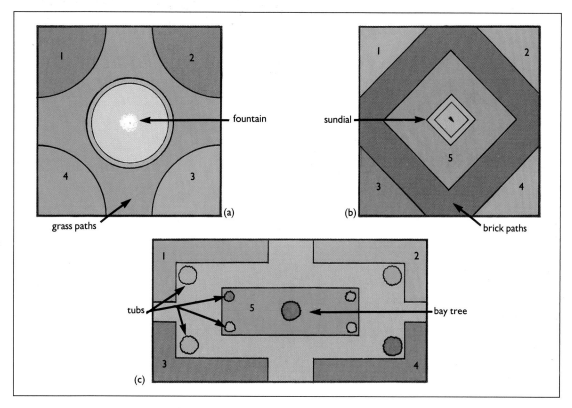

Fig 83 (a) Circles and Wedges. 1, 2, 3, 4—a selection of fragrant and ornamental herbs. (b) A plan based on triangles. 1 and 4—culinary herbs. 2 and 3—medicinal herbs. 5—ornamental herbs. (c) A plan for a garden of rectangular, raised beds. 1, 2, 3, 4—culinary herbs. 5—fragrant and colourful herbs.

fragrant garden are two obvious classifications, which certainly have their place, but there are many other ideas for interesting collections, of which the following are just a few you may wish to try.

An Anglo-Saxon Garden

Herbal charms were popular in Anglo-Saxon times to ward off disease. A garden containing the herbs listed in a poem dating from that period, The Nine Herbs Charm (which can be seen in the Harleian Manuscript in the British Museum), would make an interesting talking point. There is some disagreement amongst scholars as to the modern equivalents for the Old English names, but the nine herbs mentioned are:

Mugwort *Artemisia vulgaris* the familiar greeny-grey roadside plant.

Wegbrade This was also known as 'waybroad' and was so named because it is another common wayside plant. It is now called plantain.

Stime This is watercress. One translator suggests that the name is a reference to its fiery taste, being derived from 'stiem', meaning conflagration.

Stithe There is some confusion over this one but it is most commonly translated as a 'nettle'.

Attorlathe This is Betony, *Stachys officinalis* – a woodland plant with hairy leaves and a reddish-purple flower spike.

Maegthe This was also called 'maythem', and is camomile.

Wergulu This is crab-apple, but again this has sometimes been translated as 'nettle'.

Fig 84   *Herbs grow in wild profusion in the Anglo-Saxon garden of a Cambridge college. Familiar feverfew and pot marigold jostle with rare and elegant corn-cockle, shy opium poppies and the delicate blue flowers of flax and cornflowers. Wormwood and tansy loom large in the background.*

Fille   Variously translated as thyme and chervil.
Finule   This is fennel.

A more comprehensive Anglo-Saxon garden could include any of the plants known to be grown and used in Britain at that time. Dr Jane Renfrew, of Lucy Cavendish College, Cambridge, from her research into the subject, has compiled the following list:

Flavouring Herbs   Angelica, balm, coriander, cowslip, dill, fennel, mint, mugwort, poppy, primrose, radish, tansy, thyme, and violet.
Medicinal Herbs   Angelica, balm, cinquefoil, columbine, corncockle, cornflower, corn marigold, coriander, daisy, dill, fennel, feverfew, flax, mallow, pot marigold, meadow saffron, mint, mugwort, poppy, opium poppy, radish, strawberry and violet.
Fruits   Damson, medlar, and strawberry.
Flowers   'Apothecary's Rose', columbine, corncockle, cornflower, corn marigold, cowslip, feverfew, flax, iris, madonna lily, meadow saffron, pot marigold, primrose, and violet.
Strewing Herbs   Balm, mint, feverfew, mugwort, tansy.
Cosmetics and Perfumery   Orris root (iris), pot marigold, rose, violet, yarrow.
Dye Plants   Marigold, woad, cornflower, poppy.
Tenderizing Meat   Butcher's broom.

The herb garden at Lucy Cavendish College, designed by Dr Renfrew, is based on a simple four-bed layout and includes such romantic-sounding plants as meadow saffron, corncockle and madonna lily.

A Physick Garden

A medicinal herb, or physick garden, could include a very wide range of plants. A glance into any of the old herbals reveals that most of our native plants have been ascribed healing properties at some time. Most of the following plants could be put to use in simple home remedies and would make the basis for an attractive collection.

Elder The flowers make a soothing ointment, and the berries a drink for relieving the symptoms of a cold.
Camomile (flowers), Peppermint (leaves), Dill and Fennel (seeds) These can be made into teas with digestive properties.
Comfrey The leaves make an excellent poultice to reduce swellings. One of its old country names is 'knitbone'.
Lemon Balm, Parsley These are tonic herbs.
Lavender, Rosemary These both have antiseptic qualities. Essential oil of lavender will keep insects at bay. Rosemary is used as a heart tonic in herbal medicine.
Pot Marigold This makes ointments and infusions for chapped skin, grazes and insect bites.
Thyme This is another herb with antiseptic qualities. It is used as a gargle to combat sore throats.
Sage This is said to relieve inflamed gums and to whiten teeth.

A Shakespearean Garden

Making a garden of herbs mentioned in the works of Shakespeare could appeal to anyone with literary inclinations. The following have been referred to in the plays and sonnets:

Herbs and Flowers Bay, box, burnet, camomile, carnation, elder, fennel, honeysuckle, hys-sop, larks heels (larkspur), lavender, lily, marigold, marjoram, mint, myrtle, oxlip (primula), pansy, parsley, peony, pink, poppy, primrose, rosemary, rue, saffron (*Crocus sativus*), savory, thyme, violet, wormwood.
Roses Sweet briar (*R. eglanteria*), 'White Rose of York' (*R. Alba*), 'Red Rose of Lancaster' (*R. gallica officinalis*), cabbage rose (*R. centifolia*), damask rose and musk rose.
'Witches' Herbs (Most of which are poisonous and marked with a P) aconitum P, fern seed, hemlock P, henbane P, mandrake, opium poppy P.

A simple Shakespearean garden could take the form of a long border, backed by a wall, hedge, or trellis fence, divided into two wedge-shaped beds, with an arbour in the centre and a grass, camomile, or brick path along the front. If you have the time and space, a more formal layout, with an Elizabethan knot garden as its centrepiece, would be most appropriate.

A Tea-Garden

Herb teas are a delicious alternative to caffeine-laden conventional tea and coffee. They can be made from the fresh or dried herb. A garden of herbs for making fresh teas could be planted with any of the following:

Rosemary Put just a sprig into a cup or teapot and pour on boiling water. This tea is said to strengthen the memory, calm restlessness and dispel headaches.
Lemon Verbena This is fragrant and refreshing.
Camomile Use the flowers to make a sleep-inducing tea with digestive properties.
Peppermint This also has digestive properties.
Elderflowers Mix with camomile and peppermint for a soothing night-time drink, or for relief when you have a cold.
Lemon Balm This is said to have blood-cleansing properties, and is an excellent tea with which to start the day.

Dill, Fennel A tea made with the seeds of either of these two herbs aids digestion.

A White Garden

An ornamental garden consisting mainly of white and silver plants makes a pretty and restful feature:

Herbs with White Flowers Sweet basil, chervil, coriander, rocket, elderflower, sweet cicely, thymus album, white-flowering sage, winter savory, yarrow, and golden marjoram. 'The White Rose of York', *R. alba*, could also be included, or other old-fashioned white-flowering roses such as *Alberic Barbier*. Lily of the valley would provide early season interest and white madonna lilies could follow on.

Silver-Leaved Herbs Santolina, curry plant, wormwood, southernwood and the thymes 'Silver Posie' and 'Silver Queen'.

For maximum impact, add a contrast edging of very dark green, such as wall germander, which you should keep clipped to prevent flowering.

A Fragrant Garden

This could include the scented herbs and flowers you will need for making pot-pourri and some for beauty preparations as well.

Rose petals form the basis of most pot-pourri mixtures, so grow any of the scented and old-fashioned varieties. Other flowers for fragrance are elderflowers, camomile, bergamot, lavender and pinks. For colour, grow delphiniums, larkspur, pot marigolds and peonies, all of which can be successfully dried. Pot-pourri will be longer-

Fig 85   A white garden has an air of tranquillity.

Fig 86   A fragrant garden provides the raw
ingredients for pot-pourri.

Fig 87   A bee-skep of woven straw makes an
appropriate feature for a bee garden.

lasting and more interesting with a measure of pleasant-smelling, aromatic herbs. Mint, lemon verbena, lemon balm, pennyroyal, rosemary, marjoram, southernwood, santolina, hyssop, angelica and thyme would all be suitable.

Aromatic herbs can also be used to make fragrant bath bags. Choose mint, lemon verbena, pennyroyal, lavender, or rosemary. Put a small bunch into a small cotton bag, then hang it from the tap and allow the hot water to run through it as the bath fills.

An infusion of camomile flowers make a lightening rinse for fair hair, and rosemary, a conditioning rinse for dark hair. Sensitive skins benefit from a skin freshener made by infusing elderflowers or rose petals in distilled water.

A Bee and Butterfly Garden

A garden full of bees and butterflies encapsulates the image of high summer. Attracting these useful little creatures ensures thorough pollination of fruit, flowers and vegetables. The flowers of herbs, with their comparatively simple, single-petalled construction, are more suitable for both bees and butterflies than more elaborate garden varieties.

A bee garden should be situated in full sun-shine for maximum nectar production and in a sheltered position so that the insects are not blown about as they flit from flower to flower. A hawthorn or blackthorn hedge will provide shelter and nectar in early spring when it is most

Fig 88   A bee buries his head in 'The Apothecary's
Rose'. Bees are attracted to the uncomplicated
single-petalled structure of herb flowers.

needed. Honey-bees, with their short prob-osces, find single-petalled flowers easier to work. Bumble-bees can manage flowers with longer corollas, such as bergamot, comfrey and foxgloves.

Choose herbs to provide flowers over as long a season as possible. For early to mid-summer: bugle (ajuga), borage, chives, comfrey, marigold, nasturtiums, rosemary, sage, savory and thymes. Mid to late summer flowering species include bergamot, lemon balm, mint, lavender and sunflowers.

A Secret Garden

A most appealing garden, which makes good use of high hedging, is to be found at York gate, North Yorkshire. It is almost completely en-closed by towering hedges, which not only provide protection from the elements but add an air of mystery as the entrance affords no more than a glimpse of what is in store. It is also a garden of illusion. Only 8ft (2.4m) wide by 24ft (7.3m) long, the garden is a triumph of design and perspective, looking much more spacious

Fig 89   This herb garden is only 8ft wide by 24ft long. Clever planning and layout make it seem much more spacious.

than it really is. This effect is achieved by leading the eye up a gravel path, broken by a circular semi-paved area, to a York stone terrace and elegant, pillared pavilion. Also, instead of situat-ing the focal point – provided by a large shell on a stone plinth – centrally, it has been sited directly in front of the pavilion. Balls of golden box create an illusion of brightness and light even on the dullest of days, and the acid-green, cream and gold of variegated lemon balm, *Santolina viridis* and golden thyme add to the feeling of light and space.

A Culinary Garden

The main reason why many people grow herbs is still for their use in cookery. This category is not listed last because it is least important, but because ideas for growing culinary herbs are given throughout the book, be it in a single bed or border, in part of a larger all-purpose herb garden, in a small geometric garden, in a potager (or formal vegetable garden) or in containers.

There are just a few general observations to make concerning the layout of the culinary garden. Firstly, grow herbs for cooking near the house, as close to the kitchen door as possible. If you have to make the effort to walk to the far end of the garden when it is dark or raining to collect herbs, they will not get used. Also make sure they are accessible from a hard path. Nothing is more irritating than wading through wet grass when you have slipped out, in in-appropriate footwear, to pick a bouquet of herbs. Secondly, you must bear in mind that many of the popular culinary herbs are annuals (basil, chervil, coriander, dill, summer savory, sweet marjoram, for example), or grown as annuals (parsley). Therefore, it is more difficult to plan a scheme that stays put all the time with minimum maintenance necessary. To give the culinary herb garden structure, put perennials in strategic places, in the centre, in the corners, as edging plants, or in regularly spaced groups, leaving room for annuals to be planted around them as appropriate.

Fig 90 A culinary herb garden should always be in easy reach of the kitchen door.

DRAWING A PLAN

Even if your herb garden is to be no more than a single bed, it is a good idea to draw a plan. The finished result will be much more satisfactory than if you were to rush out, buy a selection of herbs and plant them at random. By working everything out in advance on paper, you will know exactly how many plants you will need to achieve the effect you want, and have a record of your construction material requirements, be they bricks, paving, fencing or trellis.

If you are considering a more complex design, then a carefully drawn plan, to scale, is essential. There is no mystique about drawing to scale, provided you can multiply and divide using your two times table, it is a simple matter. Use graph paper and choose a scale that will make a drawing large enough to work out detail. The

size of your design will dictate this to some extent. Obviously a 5 × 5ft (1.5 × 1.5m) border can be given a bigger scale than a garden which is 35 sq ft (3.2 sq m). 1in:2ft, or 5cm:1m, make good working scales. Graph paper comes in imperial or metric, although it has to be said that metric is easier to obtain.

If you are starting your herb garden from scratch, perhaps digging out new beds from a lawn, having measured the space available, you can decide on the final dimensions to suit your design. Draw this outline on to your graph paper. If you are using an existing bed or cultivated area, then it is essential to take accurate measurements of its outline and transfer these carefully to your diagram. Draw in any features, such as fencing or hedging, that you are going to keep, and decide whether you will need to put in a boundary enclosure; if you do, then indicate it on the plan.

If your garden is to follow a design from an existing plan or sketch (such as appear in the following pages), work out exact measurements that will fit your own plot and transfer these to the page. If, on the other hand, you have no more than a general idea of what you want, first stand on the sight and try to visualize the finished garden as you would like to see it. Picture where paths or divisions would be appropriate, and where your focal point will be. Think about where you will need height in the scheme, where you will need low-growing plants and where it would be possible to put a special feature, such as a seat, arbour or tub. Then make a rough sketch as you stand there. Use the sketch to make an accurate to-scale drawing at your leisure, at which stage you can work out the finer detail.

When it comes to planning the planting scheme, use the information you have gathered on heights and spreads to decide how much room to give each plant. Do not be tempted to cram in too much or to dot one of this and one of that about. Except where you are using one large plant as a feature (angelica, or lovage, perhaps), group plants together, planting in

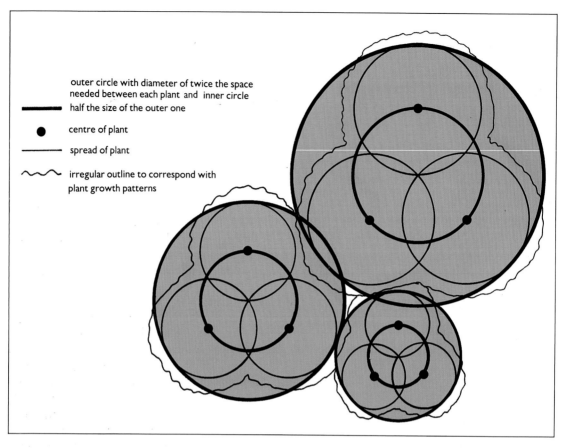

outer circle with diameter of twice the space needed between each plant and inner circle half the size of the outer one

centre of plant

spread of plant

irregular outline to correspond with plant growth patterns

Fig 91   Calculate the area that each group of plants will occupy, using a system of circles.

threes if possible. As a general rule of thumb allow about 1½–2ft (45–60cm) between larger plants, 1ft (30cm) between medium plants and 6–8in (15–20cm) between small plants. Remember that each plant grows out in all directions from its central point. Therefore, for a group of three marjoram plants, for example, you will need a circular space about 2ft (60cm) in diameter.

In order to plot the area plants will take up, taking the centre of each plant group, draw a circle on the plan which has a diameter twice the distance apart required for each plant. Then draw an inner circle half as big as the outer. There are now three points on the inner circle (representing the centre of each plant), from which to draw circles of the same diameter as the inner circle (representing the spread of each plant). A small overlap is created, ensuring the proper grouping of plants without them swamping each other (Fig 91). There is no need to plot each plant or group with this degree of precision but it is a useful procedure to follow when making initial calculations.

Now is the time, at the planning stage, to think about colours and textures so that you can decide which plants will complement each other best. The grouping of the plants will also depend on the angle from which the bed is normally seen. It might have a definite 'back' and 'front', if it is set against a hedge or wall. Mark out on the plan the areas which the plants will cover, using circles, semi-circles or, where appropriate, writing a name or key number into a complete section. You are now ready to lay out the garden.

CHAPTER 4

Laying Out the Garden

Transforming the plan into a real life herb garden is best done in stages. For a more 'instant' effect, timings can be telescoped, but the results are likely to be less satisfactory. It is well worth taking plenty of time at the preparation stage as this will save no end of work in the long run. The following is a suggested time chart:

Autumn Mark out the herb bed or garden. Dig over, de-weed, and add compost, if necessary.
Winter Lay paths and divisions, and put in boundary fencing or walls.
Spring Re-weed and put in plants.
                              OR
Spring (early) Mark out the area and dig over.
Summer Do the construction work.
Autumn Put in the plants.

As every gardener knows, the quality of the soil is the key to success. The good news is that herbs are fairly undemanding. As a general rule, they will flourish best in a light, free-draining soil, that is not too rich. However, different plants do have different requirements. Chapter 1 on Plant Profiles will guide you in this area.

Heavy clay can be very fertile and produces excellent vegetables or roses, but it is the least satisfactory for herb growing. In order to make it suitable for this purpose it will be necessary to work in plenty of bulky humus – compost or peat – and some coarse material such as grit.

Although the ideal lies somewhere between the two, a very light sandy soil is infinitely preferable to clay. It does not become waterlogged in winter, which is a condition that so many herbs, such as thyme and lavender, dislike intensely, and it warms up early in spring and is very easy to work throughout the year. The disadvantages are that in wet weather nutrients are washed through it, and it suffers badly in drought, which adversely affects such plants as angelica, bergamot, mint and lovage. For a light sandy soil it will be necessary to dig in plenty of organic matter – in the autumn or winter. Well-rotted compost or manure is ideal. This will help to retain moisture and provide the necessary nutrients. A good mulch of organic matter, applied in the spring before the soil dries out, will also help to conserve moisture, and has the added bonus of keeping weeds down.

Getting rid of perennial weeds before you start planting is a must if you are to have a trouble-free garden. Removal of persistent weeds where paths are to be laid is exceptionally important. If this is not done effectively, weeds such as couchgrass and bindweed will creep out sideways beneath the paving and become almost impossible to eradicate. The best way to get rid of weeds is to dig them out, especially the ones with deep tap-roots like hogweed, dandelion and thistle, or persistent ones with creeping underground stem systems like couchgrass, creeping buttercup and bindweed. But beware: if the least little bit of root is left behind they will spring up again, hale and hearty. Where weeds are very plentiful or well-established it may be worth using a systemic herbicide, which is absorbed by the foliage of the plant and kills by entering its sap stream.

The purpose of digging is to remove weeds and work in organic matter. It also breaks up the soil, allowing in air, which speeds up the natural

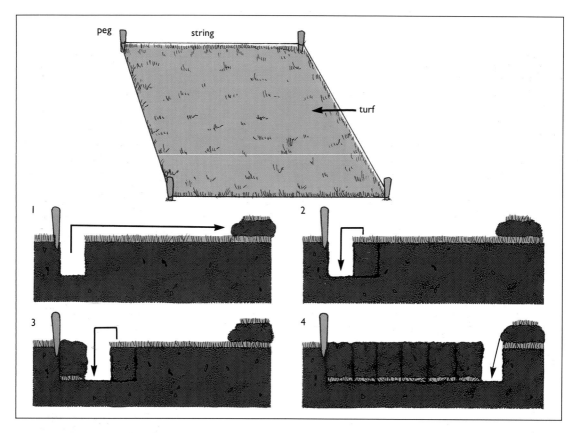

Fig 92   If an area of lawn is to be made into a herb garden, turn over the soil,
burying the turf, using a single-digging technique.

decaying process and makes nutrients available to newly planted roots. A further advantage of aerating the soil is that it encourages earthworm activity.

If you are preparing an existing border, forking it over thoroughly will probably be sufficient, once you have removed any plants that you want to move to a new home. Incorporate compost at this stage, if necessary.

Where an area of lawn is to be dug up a 'single-digging' technique is the best way to prepare it. Mark out the outline of the area to be turned into a herb garden with pegs and string. Then, start by digging out a trench about 10in (25cm) deep, or to the depth of the spade, and 10in (25cm) wide. Transport the turf and soil from this trench to the other end of the area you are digging. Then start again at one end of the opened trench, taking out another strip about

10in wide, turning it into the bit you first dug out, so burying the turf. At the same time you will be opening up a new trench. Continue like this, strip by strip until the area has been completely dug over, and the turf removed from the first trench can be used to fill the last one. If the turf is buried a full 10in (25cm) in this way, grass will not come up through the soil but will die and rot down to provide a layer of valuable humus.

For a herb garden on previously uncultivated heavy ground it may be necessary to 'double dig' it to ensure aeration to a lower level. Sandy, porous soils should not be dug too deeply. The main thing they need is an extra helping of humus in the form of compost or manure. The principle for double digging is the same as for single digging, but the trench should be double the width. Start by opening a trench 10in (25cm) deep and 2ft (60cm) wide and removing the soil

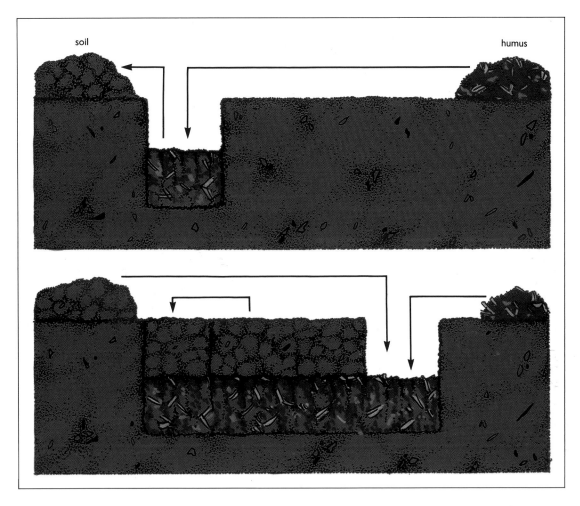

soil

humus

Fig 93   Double-digging means double the width, as much as double the depth, the lower layer being turned with a fork. It is useful for aerating a heavy soil and for adding extra humus.

to the other end of the plot. Before turning any more soil into this trench, take a garden fork and break up the soil to the full depth of the fork.

At this stage, add grit and compost. Mark out a further 2ft (60cm) width and dig the soil over into the first trench. Remove persistent perennial weeds. Shallow rooting annuals can be turned in and buried. After digging, leave the soil to settle, preferably over the winter, but at least for a week or so before planting.

After digging make sure the site is level. Raking over in several directions is enough to achieve a reasonably level surface for most purposes. However, where paths are to be laid,

and for a formal knot garden design, it is desirable to be more accurate.

TRANSFERRING YOUR PLAN TO THE GROUND

You will need: a measuring tape, pegs, a hammer to knock them in with, strong string that will not stretch too easily, and a builder's square, which you can make yourself by nailing three pieces of at least 2×1in (7×33.5cm) timber together to form a right-angled triangle, following the Pythagoras theorem, i.e., with sides in the ratio of 3:4:5.

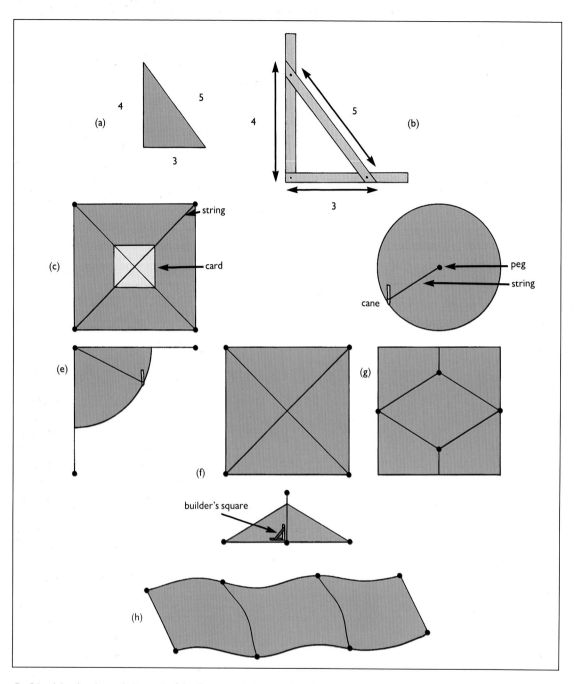

Fig 94 (a) A right-angled triangle. (b) For accurate laying out make a builder's square, based on a right-angled triangle, with sides in the ratio: 3:4:5. (c) A square can be laid out by using a piece of card as a central reference and taking lengths of string diagonally across it. (d) Marking a circle with string and cane. (e) A wedge shape. (f) Triangles formed from the diagonals of a square. Take a line at right angles from the longest side to form a flatter triangle. (g) Mark off the centres of each side of a square to form a diamond-shaped bed. (h) An informal shape can be laid out by eye, using peg and string as markers.

Laying Out Geometric Shapes

To lay out a rectangle, mark out one side, to the measurement required, with pegs and string. You may well have a fence or existing path as a boundary or guide. Using the builder's square, take the string in right angles from the corners and mark out the remaining sides, fixing the string with pegs. Check the right angles by measuring the diagonals; they should be of equal length.

A simple way to lay out a square is to lay a piece of card, cut to an accurate square, in the centre of the area to be measured. Put a peg in the centre of the card and stretch two pieces of string diagonally across it, pegging them down to form the corners. Adjust the sides to conform with the measurements of your plan.

Circles and semi-circles can be marked out by attaching a short length of cane to one end of a piece of string, measuring the same as the radius (i.e. half the diameter) of the required circle. Peg the string to the point which is to be the centre of the circle and draw round it, marking the ground with the point of the cane. Dribble sand along the impression left by the cane.

Use the corners or sides of a square, marked out with pegs and string, to form triangles, wedge shapes and diamonds. For the wedge-shape, use the string and cane method, with the corner as marker. Take diagonals across a measured square to form triangles. For a flattened-out triangle, measure the centre point of the longest side, then take a line from it at right-angles, and a line from each end of the first side to meet at a point on the central line. To form a diamond, take a measurement down from the centre of two sides of a square.

Laying Out Informal Shapes

These can also be marked out with string and pegs, adjusting them by eye until you have the shape you require. Replace the string with a dribble of sand before digging out an informal shape.

PUTTING IN DIVISIONS AND PATHS

Once you have the outline, carefully measure and mark out internal lines for paths, divisions or beds, using the techniques already described. It will usually be more convenient to replace the string with a line of sand or lime before carrying out construction work and preparing beds for planting.

In order that the soil may settle and not be trodden down and compacted it is preferable to put in paths and divisions well in advance of planting. Ideally, do the construction work over the winter months, although not of course in severe weather when the ground is frozen or snow-covered. In any case, leave it for a few weeks to settle before planting.

Hard-surface main garden paths, or wide paths in a very large herb garden are best professionally laid. Narrower paths of simple construction you may wish to tackle yourself. For all paths, a firm, level base is essential. Be very careful about laying paths, or putting in brick divisions, on ground that has been recently dug over as it will be loose and uneven. For hard-surface paths, the area should be marked out with pegs and string, then the top few inches of soil removed and the subsoil flattened and stamped to a dense hard surface. Check that it is level by putting a spirit level on a long piece of board.

For a simple brick path, spread a 2in (5cm) layer of sharp sand and cement, mixed dry (four or five parts sand to one part cement) before laying the bricks. The dry mix can be brushed into the cracks between the bricks to ensure a weed-free, even path. Over two or three weeks, the moisture in the soil will permeate the sand-cement mix and will set as concrete, holding the bricks in place. This process can be speeded up by spraying the path with the hose as soon as it is laid.

For wider paths, lay a foundation of hard core to a depth of 6–8in (15–20cm) and tamp this down firmly. Cover the hard core with a layer of sand, then bed the paving slabs or bricks with cement, checking at intervals with a spirit level on a board that the surface is even.

Trellis work, fences and brick-built boundary walls should be put in at this stage.

PLANTING

Planting can be done in autumn or spring. The advantage of autumn planting is that plants are well established by the spring and have developed a good root system to withstand summer droughts. The disadvantage is that some plants, when immature, may not stand up to winter conditions if it is very cold or the ground becomes waterlogged.

For planting out hardy, pot-raised herbs wait until the soil has warmed up a little to get them off to a good start. This will probably be about the middle of April but be guided by the particular season and the climate in which you live. Annuals can be sown straight into the ground in March or April, or started in seed-trays, potted on, then planted out in April and May. Never be tempted to plant out any half-hardy or tender herbs, or stand them outside in pots, until all danger of frost is over. This will generally be by the beginning of May in temperate climates and about three weeks later in slightly cooler areas.

If the site has been prepared and dug over in the autumn, the soil should be lightly forked over and raked before planting. Referring to the plan, stand the plants where they are to be put in. Tap each one out of its pot, dig a hole for it with a trowel and firm in well. Unless rain is likely to fall in the very near future, water in thoroughly after planting.

For summer planting, which you may want to do if you are late with your schedule or if you just want to fill in gaps, 'puddle in' plants by tipping water from a can into the planting hole before firming in the soil. Then water again and keep well watered over the following weeks until they are thoroughly established.

MAINTAINING THE HERB GARDEN

Gardens need constant tending if they are not to become overgrown and untidy. Herb gardens are no exception. Routine work includes cutting-back and weeding, watering and feeding.

Weeding

Weeds are plants that spring up in the wrong place. They compete with those under cultivation for nutrients and moisture. They also look untidy of course and are especially noticeable in a formal scheme. If the ground has been well prepared before the herb garden was laid out, the worst of the perennial weeds should have been eliminated, but some, inevitably, will find their way back and annual weeds will spring up whatever you do. Keep annual weeds under control by regular hoeing and by rooting them out before they have a chance to seed, which is not always easy!

Mulching is a useful technique for weed control and it conserves moisture in the soil into the bargain. It is essential that the ground is really wet before a mulch is applied if it is to be effective as a moisture preserver. Garden compost, chipped bark, leaf mould and spent mushroom compost can all be spread around plants. To be effective as weed suppressors, mulch must be laid 2–3in (5–7cm) thick. Roses and fruit bushes can be mulched with fresh grass clippings, which will gradually rot down and improve soil texture. Thymes, lavenders, rosemary, sage and other shrubby herbs that grow naturally in dry stony soils can be surrounded by a thin layer of gravel or shingle. This also acts as insulation, keeping the soil warm at night and cool in the day when it is hot.

For a really serious weed problem, laying black polythene around the plants is an effective treatment. It can be the only solution if, for example, you are trying to establish a new thyme bed where comfrey has been planted. Comfrey thrives on being dug up and five plants

Fig 95   *A covering of black polythene is used to suppress weeds.*

will appear in the place of one if you attempt it. Lay heavy-duty polythene over the bed, cut holes in it at intervals for the plants, making sure the openings are big enough to leave a little space around each plant for watering and to give it air. Prick holes in the polythene with a garden fork, to allow water to penetrate but which will not be large enough to allow weeds to come up. Then cover the polythene with a thick cosmetic mulch of shingle or chipped bark.

Trimming and Cutting-Back

Many herbs are wild plants and, left to themselves, they can become straggly and untidy. Frequent trimming and pruning keeps them in shape. Individual instructions are given under the entry for each plant (see Plant Profiles in Chapter 1). Southernwood and wormwood should be pruned hard in the spring to encourage fresh new growth. Other shrubby herbs, such as lavender, thyme, common sage, santolina, curry plant, hyssop, and wall germander should be cut

back after flowering. Rosemary needs careful pruning and it is best not to cut back the old wood. Herbaceous perennials, including green leafy herbs like mint and lemon balm, need cutting right back in midsummer to encourage new growth. There are, of course, many herbs which respond well to formal clipping and shaping into hedges, edges or as topiary.

Feeding

Most of the aromatic herbs thrive more if the soil is not too rich. Normal garden soil will often provide them with enough nutrients without added fertilizer. Some herbs, such as leafy green herbs for culinary use, may benefit from added nutrients. It is for the best, in the long run, to stick to organic fertilizers for all garden-grown herbs, so as not to upset the balance of nutrients in the soil. Garden compost contains some plant food, and 'fish, blood and bone' is a slow-release organic fertilizer, which contains a balance of nutrients for all purposes.

Fig 96 Comfrey is both a 'goody' and a 'baddy' in the herb garden. Although invasive, it has many uses and makes an excellent fertilizer and compost activator.

A fertilizer made from comfrey leaves can also be used for plants that need an extra boost. To make this, cut a small hole in the bottom of a plastic bucket and stand it over another container. Pack the bucket as tightly as possible with comfrey leaves, cover and leave to decay. In a few weeks, a black, tarry liquid will seep from the leaves. Dilute this with ten parts of water to one part comfrey liquid. The residue can be put on the compost heap, or used as compost itself.

A good supply of garden compost is essential in a herb garden to improve the structure of the soil, to add nutrients and to act as a mulch. There are various purpose-built bins on the market but they are quite expensive, they do not hold all that much material, and perfectly good compost can be made without them. Try to work a three-heap system so that you always have two in the making, at different stages, and one ready for use.

Reasonable compost is not difficult to make. Enclose the heap with boards or wire mesh lined with polythene, putting in two internal divisions.

Put a good mixture of materials on the compost heap. From the garden, use leaves, lawn clippings, spent vegetables, herbaceous plants that you have cut down and all the clippings from herbs. From the house, use organic waste such as vegetable peelings, tea-bags and dead flowers. Lawn clippings should not be put on in a wodge, as it makes for a slimy result, intersperse them with layers of more open-textured materials. Shredded newspaper can be added in moderation to add bulk. Woody materials are excellent but they *must* be shredded first. There are various mechanical shredders available for this job. Avoid pine needles and roots of perennial weeds (annual weeds and leaves of perennials are mostly all right but never include couch grass, bindweed or ground elder).

A compost activator helps to speed up the process of decomposition. There are various proprietary activators on the market. Comfrey leaves also make good compost heap activators. The heap should be covered to retain moisture, but see that it does not get too wet and soggy. Make sure that air can get to the compost but there really is no need to turn it. To achieve a well-rotted, crumbly compost will take about six months.

CHAPTER 5

Knot Gardens and 'Pot' Gardens

KNOT GARDENS

From medieval times, a design of interwoven lines was known as a 'knot', as were the bosses of carved wood at the intersections of ceiling beams. These may well have provided the inspiration, as well as the name, for the formal gardens of low-clipped hedges in complicated interlaced patterns.

Knot gardens first came into vogue in the early sixteenth century at the beginning of the reign of Henry VIII. They remained popular throughout the rest of the Tudor period and for most of the seventeenth century – a span of nearly two hundred years. However, during the eighteenth century, the landscape movement, with its emphasis on the 'natural' look and the ideal of rolling parkland, became the dominant influence in gardening fashion and the intricacies of the knot garden fell from favour.

Some knot garden designs, which can be seen in books of the period, are complicated in the extreme. Thomas Hyll, who published *The Gardener's Labyrinth* in 1577, included knot garden patterns that must have been exceedingly difficult to lay out and plant. The *Hortus Platinus* (1620) and *The Country Housewife's Garden* (1617) have some equally intricate designs.

From *La Maison Rustique*, translated into English by Gervase Markham in 1583, it would seem that there were two kinds of knots from the outset. The closed variety, which had interlaced threads, used plants of different shades to emphasize the interweaving. The open kind,

derived from the French *parterre*, was made up of separate beds edged with dwarf hedges. Unlike the closed variety, open knots were made to be walked within. The grand designs of André le Notre, who laid out the gardens at Versailles for Louis XIV from 1661–1668, were an important influence and the parterre gradually became the dominant form. *La Maison Rustique* decreed that ideally there should be four separate knots of different designs laid out in a square, and this configuration is seen time and again in old illustrations.

Plants recommended by early writers as being suitable for knot garden hedgings include hyssop, rosemary, wall germander, santolina and, less practically, lavender, sage, camomile, golden marjoram and thyme. However, box soon came to be the favourite, especially for the open knot, or parterre edgings, being by far the easiest to keep neat and in shape.

There is some contention as to whether the interstices were filled with coloured earths or plants but, probably, both were used, according to preference or the particular design. When infilling with earth, advantage was taken of the variety of shades provided by different types of soil, from darkest loam to yellow clay. Gravel, stones and pieces of broken coloured glass were also used. Some knots were based on heraldic devices and infilled with yellow sand, white chalk or lime, blue-tinged coal dust and crushed red bricks to reproduce the colours of heraldry. Others were filled with a variety of herbs, spring bulbs and summer flowers.

Fig 9.7 *The seventeenth-century knot garden at Hatfield House.*

Hatfield House

The extensive knot garden in front of the Old Palace at Hatfield House, Hertfordshire, is a reconstruction of a seventeenth century design and was completed in 1981. It covers an area of about 150 sq ft (13.9 sq m) and incorporates many authentic features, including four knots, or 'proportions' in varying patterns laid out in a square, with a central path in the shape of a cross. The design is based on closed knots with threads of low box infilled with flowers and herbs, all of which would have been grown in the seventeenth century. They include auriculas, borage, woodruff, pot marigolds, poppies, old varieties of dianthus, Florentine iris, martagon and madonna lilies, old-fashioned roses, sweet violets and many more.

One of the four elements is a foot maze, or labyrinth, which was a feature of gardens from the earliest of times. Such mazes were planted as allegories of the perplexities of the Christian path in life and were made not to get lost in but for contemplation.

Barnsley House

The knot garden at Barnsley House, Gloucestershire, is on a much more modest scale, having two 12 sq ft (1.1 sq m) elements. The interwoven threads are of golden and plain box and wall germander. The centre points are marked by a neatly clipped mound of *Phillyrea angustifolia* and a sphere of box. The spaces between threads and the surrounding path are filled with light-coloured gravel. At the corners, variegated hollies, clipped into standards, provide both height and interest.

(a)

(b)

(c)

Buxus sempervirens aureomarginata (variegated box)

Buxus sempervirens (box)

Teucrium chamaedrys (wall germander)

Phillyrea angustifolia

1m

0   1   2   3ft

Teucrium Chamaedrys (wall germander)

Buxus sempervirens suffritosa (dwarf box)

Buxus sempervirens (box)

Santolina chamaecryparissus (cotton lavender)

Fig 98 (a) The design of the knot garden in front of the Old Palace, Hatfield House. (b) The design of the knot garden at Barnsley House. (c) A plan of the knot garden at Hollington Nurseries.

Hollington Nurseries

At Hollington Nurseries, near Newbury, Berkshire, Simon Hopkinson has constructed a simple and most effective knot garden based on a 12ft (3.6m) square. The contrasting foliage of silver santolina, golden variegated box, dark green wall germander and lighter green ordinary box, clearly reveals the under and over pattern. To keep it in shape, the box is clipped twice a year, in May and September, and the santolina and wall germander monthly. Plants were put in at 4in (9cm) intervals and the garden took about three years to become established.

Moseley Old Hall

An example of an open knot can be seen at Moseley Old Hall, Wolverhampton. It is a reconstruction of an original design of 1640 by a Yorkshire clergyman, The Reverend Walter Stonehouse. This strikingly simple pattern is laid out entirely in dwarf box, and infilled with gravels and stones in subtly contrasting shades. In the central circular bed of each element of the design is a sphere-shaped standard box. The garden can be appreciated from an arbour walk, made of shaped timber, the design of which is based on a picture in *The Gardener's Labyrinth* by Thomas Hyll.

Creating a Knot Garden

Planning and Designing

There is no such thing as an 'instant' knot garden; you will need to plan ahead. The site must be properly prepared, the design carefully worked

Fig 99   *The striking simplicity of this design depends on the accuracy of its layout and immaculate maintenance (Mosely Old Hall).*

out, the number of plants calculated, which must then be ordered or propagated well in advance.

Designs can be made by copying the more straightforward seventeenth-century patterns, or by adapting and simplifying complicated ones. Alternatively, using ruler and compasses, you can make up your own design based on a combination of straight lines and semi-circles. Once you have decided on the pattern, draw it to scale on squared paper.

The next thing to do is to decide on the planting plan. Mark it on the design using a colour code. Then work out how many you will need of each variety, calculating this on a basis of planting at intervals of a minimum of 4in (9cm) and a maximum of 6–8in (15–20cm). If you are propagating your own plants you will need to start box cuttings two years in advance. Allow at least one year for santolina, and for wall germander six months.

Knot gardens were intended to be looked down on from above so that the intricacies of the pattern showed to advantage, so try and choose a site where your knot can be viewed from a vantage point above. Perhaps you could make use of different levels in the garden, a terrace, or a sunken garden. Or you may be able to ensure that it can be appreciated from a first floor window, as were so many of the gardens of old.

If you are planning to plant in the spring, prepare the area the previous autumn. Dig it over well, eradicating weeds by rooting out every scrap. Alternatively, treat with a systemic herbicide. Box hedging takes goodness from the soil and has a drying effect. As there will not be the chance to dig the site over again once it has been planted, incorporate plenty of good garden compost at this stage, especially if you intend to fill interstices with other plants.

It really is essential that the ground should be absolutely level. Lumps and bumps that would hardly notice in an ordinary border are disastrous in a formal planting and would spoil the whole effect. Given a reasonably flat piece of ground, careful digging and raking should be quite sufficient, provided you leave it to settle and compact for as long as possible. If you have a particularly difficult area to deal with, or are in any doubt as to whether it is even, check it with a spirit level on short lengths of flat board.

A very simple design, based on straight lines and semi-circles, can be marked out using peg and string. First establish a square, using a builder's square for the right angles, or a square card with string stretched diagonally across it. Then draw in the semi-circles with a piece of cane tied to a string of the required length, fixed to a central peg.

A more complicated pattern can be transferred to the ground with a grid system. This is the method suggested in the seventeenth century gardening manual, *La Maison Rustique*, and is still the best way to mark out a knot garden design, of any complexity, accurately. Using pegs and string, lay a grid over the desired area. This can be used as a guide to mark out the curves. Draw them in free hand with a pointed cane, rubbing out errors and re-marking as necessary, or cut templates of card or stiff polythene, using a felt-tip pen and strong scissors. The next thing to do is to lay these on the grid, drawing round with a cane and re-positioning as necessary to make up the pattern.

Once you have the design to your satisfaction, dribble fine sand or, preferably, garden lime as it is longer lasting, over the lines as a planting guide.

Planting

Planting can be done in spring or early autumn. As discussed in Chapter 4 there are advantages and disadvantages to both, so do whichever is most convenient for you. If you decide to plant in summer, avoid very dry spells and be prepared to water copiously unless the season is exceptionally wet.

Sprinkle the area lightly with blood, fish and bone (organic fertilizer) a few days before planting and fork it in lightly. Keeping very strictly to the lines you have marked out, make little holes with a trowel and put the plants in at 6in (15cm)

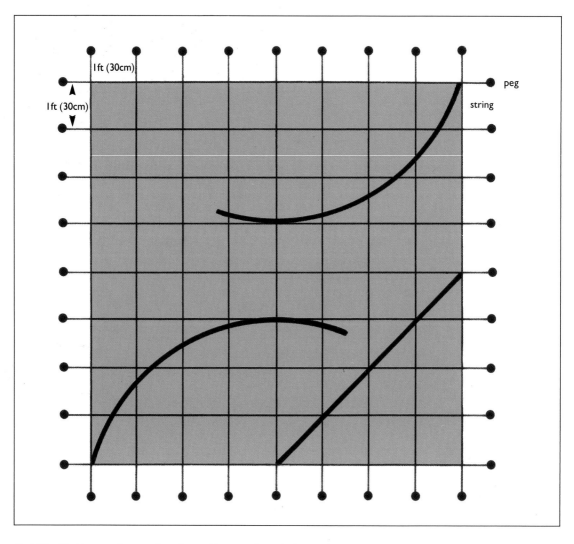

Fig 100   Marking out a knot garden using a grid system. Draw the lines with a
sharp pointed cane, going over them with sand or lime.

intervals, or slightly closer if you wish to achieve a dense effect quickly. Tread in firmly and water well after planting. If you have planned an ambitious garden you might not be able to plant it out in one session. This does not matter; it is better to do it slowly and accurately than rush the job and get things out of line.

Wall germander is the easiest of plants. With box, it is as well to keep spares of the same height and age, in case of failures in the early stages which will leave unsightly gaps. If the knot is to be infilled with herbs, let the little hedges develop for a season before putting in all the filling plants, although you may like to plant important groupings or clumps, central to the design, at the outset. Coloured gravels or earth can be laid immediately, and these will help with weed control.

Maintenance

Do not let weeds develop strong roots and get a hold; pull them out as soon as you see them. If you have prepared the site thoroughly, weeds should not be too much of a problem but, inevitably, some will appear until the plants fill out. The other major task is clipping. Box will grow more slowly than the others, but it is important to cut it regularly to keep a good shape, twice a year in May and September is recommended. Cut other herbs back as often as they begin to look straggly or outgrow the line of the hedge. This will be three to four times a year, with a hard cut in early spring to encourage bushy growth. For knot gardens infilled with other herbs, rather than gravels, be equally firm. Do not let them sprawl and overpower the scheme, but keep well cut back. Be ruthless about rooting out plants that have become old or straggly and replace them.

THE POTAGER OR 'POT' GARDEN

The French influence on British gardening fashion in the sixteenth and seventeenth centuries was considerable. Just as the parterre became the model for the ornamental garden, the 'potager', set out in neat geometric patterns, was the inspiration behind the formal kitchen garden, or 'pot garden', as it was often called at that time.

At the beginning of this period, kitchen gardens predominately contained plants that we would call herbs. In fact, no distinction was made between herbs and vegetables. Edible herbs and vegetables alike were known as 'pot herbs', 'salad herbs' or 'roots', according to type. The word 'vegetable' only came to be used in its current sense in the late eighteenth century. In his chapter on 'herbs and roots for the kitchen' in *The Gardener's Labyrinth*, Thomas Hyll lists leeks, onions, shallots, cabbage, spinach, beets and asparagus along with orache, rocket, parsley, sorrel, chervil, sage, hyssop, thyme, marjoram, lavender, rosemary, southernwood, savory, costmary, basil, balm and camomile. Directions for planting suggest that some beds contained a single species and in others several different herbs were grown together.

It is sometimes said that the ornamental potager is a demanding and time-consuming way

Fig 101   *A long bed of chives contained by a dwarf box hedge. Flowers grow in abundance amongst the vegetables in this beautiful potager.*

to grow vegetables. If you are aiming for a show garden of precision standards in a complicated design, then it would be a daunting task to take on. However, carried out on a modest scale, without striving for total symmetry, it is the most rewarding kind of garden you could hope to have. From a practical view point, vegetables grow much better surrounded by plenty of aromatic herbs and are far less troubled by pests and diseases. Also, it is so much less soul-destroying to cultivate a few choice vegetables in a little square bed, bordered by a brick path, rather than having to tend long rows of produce, whilst balancing on one of those unwieldy planks beloved of television gardeners. As to quantitites, a small ornamental potager is better geared to the needs of the average household of two to four, than most conventional vegetable gardens, half of the produce from which has to be given away.

A potager is not only practical, it is also pretty. It is the ideal choice for those who would like some home-grown produce, as well as herbs, but are reluctant to give up valuable garden space to a dull and unattractive vegetable patch.

The Potager at Villandry

The grounds of this Renaissance chateau contain the supreme example of an ornamental kitchen garden. It is justly world-famous. The gardens at Villandry are a recreation of those laid out in the sixteenth century, and the potager is, in turn,

based on the monastic gardens, first planted on the same site in the Middle Ages. The dominant cross motif, repeated in single and double form, dates from this earlier period, as does the inclusion of the many roses.

The overall design consists of nine square plots each made up of a different geometric pattern. The colours of the vegetables and their leaves are carefully chosen to emphasize the pattern. The present-day planting is based on vegetables known and used in sixteenth-century France. The range by then had increased considerably, from the few (mainly cabbages, leeks and carrots) that the monks would have planted alongside their herbs. The beds are edged with box and the borders surrounding them are filled with spring and summer flowers to provide colour and interest, an idea with which Thomas

Fig 102   The bright colours of flowers attract beneficial insects to the vegetable garden.

Fig 103   *The potager at Villandry provides a standard of excellence which is an inspiration. All vegetables used in the planting schemes at Villandry were available in sixteenth-century France.*

Fig 104   *It is less daunting to cultivate vegetables grown in compact blocks than in seemingly endless rows.*

Hyll was familiar. He recommends planting 'pleasant flowers' in the kitchen garden for their 'delectable sight'.

The gardens at Villandry take a great deal of planning and organization. There are two major plantings per year, one for spring and one for summer vegetables. As well as aesthetic considerations and colour contrasts, there is the rotation of crops to take into account. (Vegetables of the same family should not be grown on the same piece of ground in consecutive years and a three-year cycle is recommended.)

The sheer scale of the operation at Villandry takes it out of the realm of the ordinary domestic garden. It is maintained by six full-time gardeners, with extra seasonal back-up, and the publicity literature is full of breath-taking statistics on the number of plants propagated, the miles of hedging clipped, the many man-hours involved, and the acreage covered – the potager covers 3 acres (1.3 hectares) of the overall 17 acre (6.9 hectare) site. However, it does provide a wealth of ideas.

Barnsley House

At Barnsley House in Gloucestershire, Rosemary Verey has created an ornamental potager on a more modest scale than the one at Villandry. Adapted from a design by William Lawson in *The Country Housewife's Garden* (1617), it makes a more accessible model for the average gardener.

The four main elements of the design are delineated by paths of different-coloured bricks, laid in varying patterns. Scent is provided by lavender which borders some of the paths, and by the old-fashioned standard roses at the corners of the central diamond. Domes of golden box underline the sense of order and formality. Cabbages and onions grow in disciplined blocks and there is plenty of colour from a variety of flowers, such as chicory, evening primrose, and sunflowers.

Creating a Potager

Planning and Designing

Creating a potager is a rewarding project, which needs a little planning, but is easy to achieve if

Fig 105   *The ornamental potager at Barnsley House.*

build-up of disease and depletion of soil nutrients. There is no need to be too rigid about this, as in a small space a strict pattern of rotation is not always practicable, but do not grow the same vegetable crop on the same spot year after year. This applies especially to members of the cabbage and carrot families, which are susceptible to disease and insect infestation. Onions can be grown on the same ground in successive years, and so can beans, but it is still preferable to move them about from time to time. When filling in your planting plan, make three versions, to cater for a three-year cycle.

Put in the paths well ahead of planting, preferably in the previous autumn, so that the soil around them is not trodden and compacted when it comes to sowing seeds and setting out plants.

Good vegetables require good soil, rich in nutrients and moisture. They will *not* thrive on a 'poorish' soil, unlike many herbs. Therefore, dig the site over thoroughly and incorporate plenty of manure or well-rotted garden compost, using the single-digging technique described on page 92. This is especially necessary where you plan to grow beans. Leave the plot to overwinter after digging. In the spring, remove any weeds and lightly fork in fish, blood and bone (slow-release organic fertilizer) before planting.

Planting

Put in the permanent feature plants first. This can be done in autumn. Plant roses, if these are to be included, in winter, when they are dormant. Container-grown roses can, in theory, be put in all year round, but be very careful about planting in a dry spell unless you are prepared to water copiously. Sow vegetable seeds in a greenhouse or cold frame, starting in March, transplanting in April or May as appropriate, or buy in young vegetable plants from the garden centre as required. To avoid bare patches for long periods, aim for a second successional planting where necessary. Quick maturing crops, such as radishes, are useful fillers.

tackled in stages. An existing vegetable patch makes an ideal site but it could take centre stage in the middle of the front lawn if you prefer.

As with all effective garden design, the first thing to do is to stand on the site and picture the possibilities. Next, measure accurately the space you have available and draw the outline on to a piece of squared paper. Then sketch in the main paths and divisions as appropriate, basing them, if you like, on an old print. However, if you do not have much space, keep the design very simple. Allow for some permanent features and planting, such as thyme or lavender edgings, fruit bushes and roses, leaving plenty of gaps for annual herbs and vegetable crops.

Vegetables should be rotated to prevent

CHAPTER 6

Growing Herbs in Containers

GROWING HERBS OUTSIDE

It is not necessary to have a large garden, or indeed a garden at all, to grow herbs. One of the most satisfactory ways of cultivating them is in

Fig 106   An exceptionally fine standard bay tree in a large stone pot makes a dramatic feature on the terrace.

pots. A sunny courtyard or patio, roof-garden, balcony or window-box could all be put to use for this purpose. A mixed tub or a group of pots, in varying sizes and styles, planted with herbs chosen for their useful, fragrant or decorative properties according to preference, makes a self-contained herb garden.

However, there are many ways in which containers come into their own. They can camouflage unsightly elements, like drain covers, give height to a bed or border, become the central feature in a design, or provide punctuation. A few strategically placed pots give form to a herb garden. A grand pot containing a feature plant can stand alone on a terrace or several can be arranged in formation.

Containers are useful for growing herbs where the soil is unsuitable, perhaps because it is heavy and difficult to work or exceptionally dry and impoverished, as it often is in town gardens. Also, in gardens where there is no convenient bed or patch of soil in the right place, a paved area by the back door is the ideal place for a tray of mint or pot of chives.

Some plants are actually better grown in containers. This goes for half-hardy and tender plants, including lemon verbena, scented pelargoniums and pineapple sage. They can then be moved into protection for the winter (remember that all container-grown plants are more vulnerable to frost than if planted out in the soil). It is also more practical to grow formally clipped box or bay in containers. They do not seem to mind root restriction and will grow happily in

Fig 107   Wooden tubs planted with aromatic and colourful herbs (the blue flowers are flax and the yellow, dyer's camomile) are used to camouflage unsightly drain covers.

pots for years. The more 'difficult to raise' herbs, such as basil and parsley, and those which resent transplantation, such as chervil, will often do better in pots as they can be given optimum growing conditions.

Most of the favourite culinary herbs flourish in pots and make a popular choice for container gardens. The most suitable ones are bay, basil, chervil, chives, coriander, dill, mint, parsley, marjoram, savory, tarragon and thyme.

Ornamental herbs for containers include the many ornamental thymes, silver-leaved herbs, such as santolina and curry plant, variegated forms of mint and the fragrant bergamot mint. Colourful flowering herbs are also good subjects for pots, including bright and easy-to-grow pot marigolds, nasturtiums, pinks, and low-growing lavenders, such as 'Hidcote' and 'Munstead'.

Herbs to avoid are those that grow very large and have deep roots, such as angelica, lovage and fennel. Then there are some that are not worth the effort and look more effective planted in groups in the garden. Borage and bergamot come into this category. Restriction of the roots of large, shrubby plants, like rosemary and sage, dwarfs them. They may do quite well for a while, but are likely to become straggly quickly. However, they can be a good choice so long as you view them as short-term prospects, which will need re-potting or renewing frequently.

Containers

A wide choice of pots and containers is available. Many are made of some form of plastic. This is a practical material for the purpose, being lightweight, durable and cheap, but not the most attractive. Inexpensive pots made of moulded, recycled cellulose, are also on the market in sizes suitable for patio planting, but these are not nearly as durable as plastic and, with their corrugated cardboard appearance, not to everyone's taste as far as looks go either.

Terracotta pots look the part for a container herb garden. They come in a wide choice of design, from the smallest and simplest to enormous elaborate urns and jars, and the rich colour sets off most herbs to perfection. They can be expensive and they are also breakable but, if aesthetics are your priority, they must be top choice. Purpose-made terracotta herb pots, sometimes called strawberry pots, with holes or

Fig 109   A stone trough planted with creeping thyme.

pockets in the sides, can be planted with a mixture of herbs, or with several forms of one species such as thyme. The smaller versions can be used for parsley.

Stone urns and troughs are also tops for looks. They may not be as versatile as pots, which you can move about but, with their natural colour and texture, they are in keeping with the spirit of a herb garden and make wonderful features. Wooden tubs and troughs can be rustic and strike the right note in an informal cottage-style herb garden. If painted, they can be very formal and elegant as are the traditional square box-shaped tubs used for ornamental bays. Wood is also the material frequently used for window-boxes, which can make most effective herb gardens. Look out for unusual containers. Barrels, chimney pots and stone sinks planted with suitable herbs, brighten up a dull corner or make interesting centre-pieces.

Drainage

The key factors in a successful container herb garden are drainage and watering. Inadequate

Fig 108   The richness of terracotta sets off the green simplicity of herbs to perfection. The grand scale of this urn is emphasized by the smaller pots at its base.

111

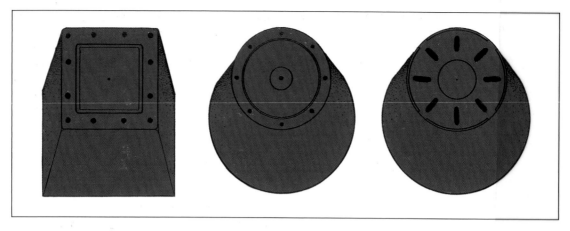

Fig 110   The pot in the centre has inadequate drainage holes, which should be enlarged before planting.

drainage is one of the most common reasons for failure, especially with large containers, such as window-boxes. Unless they are free-draining, the compost becomes waterlogged and sour and the roots of the plants rot. Before planting, check the drainage holes in plastic pots. Some may not have been punched through and some are too small, in which case punch out some extra, larger ones. With good drainage holes, a base layer of broken crocks is not usually necessary in plastic pots. As terracotta pots are porous, inadequate drainage is less likely. This type of pot usually has one large hole in the bottom. To prevent this clogging up, it is a good idea to cover it with broken crocks before filling with compost. Ensure that wooden tubs and troughs have been drilled with drainage holes. They can be lined with black polythene (which has also been pierced with holes) to protect the wood. Spreading a layer of coarse gravel in larger tubs and troughs before topping up with potting compost, also helps drainage.

Composts

Never use ordinary garden soil in your containers. It will harbour pests, diseases and weeds, lack the right balance of nutrients and is likely to be of unsuitable texture for drainage. In the confines of a pot, it is essential to provide as perfect and pampering an environment as possible.

There are two basic kinds of potting composts available: peat-based and loam-based. Peat-based composts (sometimes referred to as 'soilless') retain moisture better than the loam-based ones, although they are difficult to re-wet if they are allowed to dry out completely. Peat composts are also not so heavy, which makes them suitable for hanging baskets or for pots that may need moving about. Herbs that need plenty of moisture, which includes basil, pineapple sage, mints and parsley, are better in peat-based composts. Loam-based composts, with their free-draining, more open texture, suit other herbs better. Thymes, lemon verbena, bay, scented pelargoniums and lavender do better in a loam-based compost. If you do want to use peat-based compost for these herbs, add grit or perlite, in the proportion of one part of grit to five parts compost, to achieve a more open-textured medium.

Plants make different demands on compost at different stages of development. For germinating seeds and establishing cuttings, a compost with the minimum of nutrients is required. At this stage, moisture and circulation of air are the main considerations. Once the plants start to grow, they need more nourishment, whilst mature plants, confined to one pot for any length of time, need more still. Proprietary composts are graded to suit these varying requirements. Peat-based composts come in a 'seed and cuttings' and a 'potting' formulation. There is also an 'all-purpose' grade, intended, as its name suggests, for starting seeds and cuttings, growing plants on and even for use in pots where plants have to make a permanent home. With extra feeding it seems adequate for this last purpose.

Planting

It should be taken into account that container-growing is, in general, a short-term project. Mixed containers will need replanting every year. Some that are planted with a single variety may last a little longer, but should be re-potted when they seem pot-bound and growth becomes poor. A few, which contain feature plants, and are kept for many years, such as bays, should be re-potted every few years, either to give them more room or to provide them with a completely fresh supply of compost.

The size of container you choose will depend on the size of plant you put in it, or the number of plants you intend to include. There are no hard and fast rules here. Clearly it is a matter of common sense and knowing your plants.

Restricting the roots of naturally large plants forces them to grow in a dwarf form. Some will take to this treatment more readily than others. Bay, for example, is very slow-growing and will tolerate a small pot for longer and take root restriction better than lemon verbena. If you buy one of these potentially large plants when small and immature, it should not go straight into the biggest pot you can find. Pot it on gradually from year to year but, each time, into something no more than two sizes larger. This is a general rule to follow when potting and re-potting. Never be tempted to try and save time by setting out a tiny plant straight from a seed-tray into a 9in (23cm) pot, which you have chosen as its final home; it

will not flourish. Prick it out into a 3in (8cm) pot and let it develop first before potting on.

On the other hand, if they are going to reach their full potential, plants need space to develop. Bear this in mind when potting on annuals, or herbs grown as annuals, such as basil and parsley. However, for a dense show of pot marigolds, they should be closely packed together in a medium pot. If you give them too much space and rich compost, the leaves will develop at the expense of the flowers. As a general guide, allow a 9in (23cm) pot for one basil plant, and a tub of at least 12in (30cm) in diameter and 9in (23cm) deep if you put three in together. Chives would have room to thrive in a 9in (23cm) diameter and 6in (15cm) deep pot. Divide and re-pot annually. Tarragon, with its creeping root system also needs a medium pot and dividing annually. Mint will do well in various sizes of container. For a good supply, set out cuttings at 3in (7cm) intervals in a trough 22in (56cm) long by 7in (18cm) wide and 5in (14cm) deep. Replant each year, teasing out the tangled roots and dividing. Thyme can be kept in anything from a 6in (15cm) pot upwards, depending on the variety, and how much you want it to develop. It will often stay in the same pot for several years.

Grouping

Container-grown plants thrive when the pots are massed together. Grouped plants are easier to water and in hot weather they benefit from the moisture provided by neighbouring leaves and damp compost. They look their best this way too. Troughs or tubs containing a mixture of herbs are popular and the ideal solution if space is limited. They can look very effective but, as the plants will be packed together, competing for moisture and nutrients, extra attention must be paid to watering and feeding. In a mixed planting, put the taller-growing herbs to the centre of a tub and fill round with lower-growing or creeping varieties. In a trough, if it is too narrow to plant taller herbs to the back, put them in the centre with the smaller ones to each side.

Fig 111   Plants thrive when grouped closely together. In this 'all-purpose' container garden, scented pelargoniums and lemon verbena are at the back, with dill, parsley, pot marigold, and sweet basil (centre). In the front are bay, variegated applemint, bergamot mint, thyme and purple basil.

Avoid larger shrubs, such as lemon verbena, or very thirsty plants, such as pineapple sage. It is safer, on the whole, to stick to medium and small herbs for mixed plantings.

Culinary Collections   A trouble-free mixed trough of culinary herbs could include marjoram, thyme, tarragon, winter savory, parsley and chives. Herbs can also be kept in their separate pots within the trough. This can be useful if you want to ring the changes without replanting the whole trough and makes it easy to fill gaps if a plant dies. It is also quite a good way to keep mint from overpowering its neighbours.

Ornamental Collections   There is plenty of scope for the imagination. A silver collection could be based on rosemary and 'Silver Posie' thyme, with deep pink dianthus and rich purple lavender for colour contrast. Golden sage looks wonderful with santolina and curry plant. Hyssop planted in a tub with pot marigold is an easy-going combination that needs little attention. Purple basil, chives, and southernwood with the multi-coloured *Ajuga reptans* creeping over the side of the pot provides plenty of contrast in colour and texture. A selection of mints with different-coloured foliage, planted together and allowed to mingle can also be very eye-catching.

A mixed thyme collection is one of the best ways of using those custom-made herb or strawberry planters, with pockets in the sides. When the thymes are in flower, this makes a wonderful, colourful feature, and the different shades of foliage give it a long season of interest. They can also be filled with mixed culinary herbs. Choose medium-sized herbs, of similar growth, if possible, to avoid an unbalanced planting. Herbs have to live in cramped conditions in these containers, and it is difficult to water them thoroughly, so always replant each year, with new stock and fresh compost. Smaller versions of herb planters can be used for parsley.

Planting a Parsley Pot

Parsley pots and mixed herb pots look decorative but, from the plants' point of view, they can be stressful. Roots are often cramped and water supplies do not always seep right through the potting medium. When choosing a parsley pot, make sure there are not too many holes and that they are of adequate size. The strawberry pot kind, with lipped pockets, is the best one to go for.

Put a few broken crocks in the bottom and fill to the level of the first pocket with a peat-based compost. Tap it down well and press in lightly, without compacting the compost. Separate parsley seedlings and put one in the first cavity, working from the inside outwards, so that the roots lie flat and are not damaged by pushing them through a hole. Fill in with soil to the height of the next pocket. Continue in this way until all

Fig 112   Planting a parsley pot.   (a) Choose a pot that does not have too many holes. The one on the left is of preferable design to the pot on the right.   (b) Fill to the level of the first hole with compost.   Avoid damaging the roots, by pushing the leaves of seedlings through the hole, working from the inside.

the pockets are filled, using one seedling per cavity. Water from the top using a fine-rosed can. To ensure that it is moist through, you should stand the pot in a tray or saucer filled with water so that it is soaked up from the base as well. Remember to keep well watered and, once the plants begin to develop, feed sparingly, about once per week will be sufficient. Use the same technique when planting an ornamental thyme pot or a mixed herb pot.

Hanging Baskets

A herbal hanging basket can make a most unusual feature but it is quite difficult to keep the plants looking in peak condition for any length of time. Most of the medium-sized herbs can be included. Mint and creeping thymes are useful for the trailing effect necessary in a hanging basket. Simple combinations often work best, such as rue, 'Jackman's Blue' variety, with ordinary

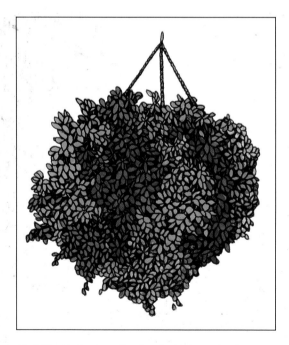

Fig 113   Herbs planted in a hanging basket make an unusual, fragrant feature for a patio or doorway. Simple combinations of plants work best.

sage, purple sage and tricolour sage, or golden marjoram with golden thyme and winter savory. Lavender and hyssop with pinks, and plenty of creeping thyme trailing from the sides is another good combination.

A hanging basket can be planted entirely with one species, such as parsley or winter savory, spacing the plants all round through gaps in the liner, to form a ball of foliage. Plant closely and put plenty of plants in the sides of the basket. A peat compost, containing slow-release fertilizer should be used. Water frequently – at least once a day and in warmer weather twice – and feed weekly.

Maintenance

Unlike indoor plants, which are often killed by 'kindness' or, at any rate, by too much water through the winter when they are dormant, it would be difficult to overwater herbs grown outside in pots through the summer. As a general rule, give them plenty of water at a time and let them almost dry out before re-watering to ensure they do not get waterlogged. The smaller the pot, and bigger and faster-growing the plant, the more quickly it will dry out and need re-watering. Some herbs have a greater requirement for water than others. The ones with needle-shaped leaves, thymes and rosemary, for example, are adapted to take less water than others. Pineapple sage, on the other hand, cannot get enough. In hot weather, a large specimen will need at least a gallon, twice a day. Basil, needing to be kept moist, comes in between these extremes.

The supply of nutrients in a pot is limited because of the space and because they are leached away in watering. This means that herbs which may do very well in the garden without extra fertilizer, because they can make new roots to draw on the wider supplies available, will need feeding if kept in pots. The more you have to water, the quicker nutrients will be leached away.

All plants need a mixture of nitrogen for leaves, phosphates for roots, and potash for flowers, plus some trace elements. There are a number of plant foods on the market which contain these components. Choose one that can be applied in liquid form. There should be sufficient nutrient in the compost for the first month after potting. Thereafter, during the growing season, feed about once a week, depending on the particular plant's requirements and the frequency of watering. Follow the instructions on the packet or bottle exactly and do not assume that more means better. The results of too much fertilizer are stunted growth and wilting leaves, which are sometimes spotted or edged with brown. Too little fertilizer can also result in stunted, slow growth, but more obvious signs are pale, yellowing leaves and weak stems.

The main reason for growing culinary herbs is in order to harvest them. This can only do good

as it will encourage bushy growth and keep plants in shape. However, allow them to become established before you start to pick them. As with herbs grown in garden soil, it is important to prevent flowering if a good supply of leaf is to be maintained. This is especially relevant to basil, which should have the tips pinched out at frequent intervals.

Ornamental herbs that are not being regularly harvested will benefit from trimming. Cut back thymes, lavender and hyssop after flowering, and santolina and curry plant as soon as they become straggly. Pot-grown rosemary and ordinary garden sage need only light trimming, once a year, in early spring. Ornamental sages, 'Icterina', purple and tricolour, should be cut back in the autumn and kept in frost-free protection. Lemon verbena should be cut back hard in the autumn once the leaves begin to fall. Pineapple sage will benefit from being cut back

Fig 114   Slow-growing bay trees are well suited to containers.

to base, after it has flowered, which will be from October to December, depending on the amount of heat it has. Plants do need a dormant time so, even if you keep them in a greenhouse through the winter, allow them to rest by not feeding and only water very sparingly.

GROWING HERBS INDOORS

Growing herbs indoors is not entirely satisfactory. They will be deprived of sufficient light, air and humidity, and large patio pots and urns, which provide plants with space for root development, are impractical. One solution to the unfriendly environment problem is to give indoor herbs a turn outside, alternating them with a second set.

Culinary Herbs

The main reason for growing culinary herbs in the house is to have a fresh supply conveniently to hand. With this as the objective, herbs can be kept in medium-sized pots, cropped frequently and replaced as necessary. Do not expect to keep the same plant going year after year, even if it is a perennial. Perennials will have a shorter life than if grown under more natural conditions.

The kitchen window-sill is the most popular place for keeping a fresh herb supply. It is also the most practical, and can provide a relatively suitable environment. Lighting should be adequate and the atmosphere in a kitchen is likely to be moister than in the rest of the house.

Do not expect to keep a supply of fresh herbs going all through the winter. Once annuals have completed their life-cycle, they should not be replanted in mid-winter as light levels will be too low for sustained healthy growth. Perennials, even though they may keep their leaves all year round, need a resting period during which feeding should be stopped and watering greatly reduced. As they will not be putting on new growth at this time, only very limited picking is practical. Bearing these points in mind the same

range of herbs recommended for outdoor pot growing is suitable. The ones you select will depend on individual preference. A comprehensive selection would include those delicate-textured herbs for use in non-cooked dishes and the components of the classic combination *fines herbes*, parsley, chervil, chives and tarragon; bay, thyme, marjoram and winter savory, which are robust, warm-tasting herbs, used mainly in cooked dishes; and basil and mint for their inimitable flavours.

Chervil can be successfully sown at six to eight week intervals, and harvested straight from the tray. Parsley could be grown two to three plants in a 6in (15cm) pot, or in a special parsley-pot with holes. Chives and tarragon can be kept in 6in (15cm) pots, if replaced frequently. Basil will need a slightly bigger pot – around 8in (20cm) – if it is to last the season. If you pinch out the tips to make it bushy and do not allow it to flower, it will keep going until Christmas. Grow mint in a container that is large enough to give space to the roots. After a summer's use, cut it back, divide and repot in January.

Of all the culinary plants grown indoors, bay is the one to keep the longest. Repot annually, or at least every two years, using a compost with plenty of grit in it. Do not keep it too wet and stand it outside for a few months during the summer. Thyme and winter savory could last for a year or two if given an outdoor break. Repot as necessary into a pot that is one size larger. Take some cuttings in the second year to provide replacement plants, or grow some on from seed. Marjoram should be prevented from flowering in order to provide plenty of leaf throughout the season. Divide and re-pot in the second year.

Secrets of Success

Keeping herbs in individual pots is the easiest way to control and maintain them. Stand the pots on saucers, clustered together, as they seem to grow better in close contact with each other.

Fig 115 *Scented pelargoniums make lovely house-plants. Left to right:* P. tomentosum, P. crispum variegatum *and* P. capitatum.

Once again, drainage and correct watering are the keys to success. To ensure good drainage, put pots on a layer of damp gravel in a tray or plant trough. This will provide humidity without giving the plants 'wet feet'. Check that all pots have good drainage holes. A free-draining compost is essential, especially for shrubby perennials such as rosemary, sage, winter savory and thyme. If you use a peat-based compost, mix in extra grit or coarse sand. Be careful not to overwater. Plants will not dry out as quickly as if they were kept in the sun on the patio. Basil, mint and, to a lesser extent, parsley and chervil, need to be kept moist most of the time but never soaking wet, which will only encourage weakness and rot. For most other herbs, allow the compost to dry out almost completely before re-watering.

Ornamental and Fragrant Herbs

Some of the aromatic herbs can be grown quite successfully as house-plants. Any of the scented-leaved pelargoniums are ideal for this purpose. They do not mind dry conditions and relatively low light levels. They will grow quite prolifically and need staking and plenty of judicious trimming in autumn and early spring to keep them in check. Alternatively, put one on a plant-stand or jardinière and let the foliage cascade downwards.

Pineapple sage can be allowed to flourish and develop outside during the summer months, and can then be brought in in early September. If you keep it in as light a place as possible and give it plenty of water you will be rewarded with a lovely show of red flower spikes in October or November. Rosemary and lemon verbena can also be grown indoors. The general rules for looking after house-plants apply; keep them in a cool, light position, away from draughts, water well and feed regularly through the summer. Allow them to have a dormant or resting period through the winter. Lemon verbena will lose its leaves in the winter but new growth will come through in the spring.

CHAPTER 7

Pests and Diseases

Herbs are, on the whole, less vulnerable to pests and diseases than other groups of plants. This is thought to be because many of them contain strong, aromatic oils which have anti-bacterial, insect repellent properties. Thyme, lavender, rosemary, and scented pelargoniums, for example, are seldom troubled by pests. Many other strong-smelling herbs, such as rue, santolina, curry plant, pennyroyal and tansy, are also unlikely to suffer, whilst chives and garlic, grown on a garden scale, are remarkably resistant to pests and diseases. All these herbs, moreover, are useful insect repellents in themselves. If planted nearby, they will help to provide a measure of protection for softer-leaved, less strong-smelling herbs, which are more vulnerable to attack.

The same principle can be applied when growing vegetables. Marigolds help to keep tomatoes free from pests and a row of summer savory surrounding a broad bean patch will deter, although it will not completely eliminate, blackfly.

However, from time to time, pest and disease problems do arise in the herb garden. The ones you are most likely to encounter are listed below.

PESTS

Caterpillars

These sometimes go for the young leaves of basil, the annual, sweet marjoram, and summer savory. Dusting with derris powder acts as a deterrent.

Fig 116   Caterpillars find young basil leaves tasty. Grow it in pots to deter them.

Slugs and Snails

The very small grey and black slugs are the worst culprits. They attack the same plants as caterpillars, and also young bergamot shoots. Unless you want to spend half the night picking them off by torchlight and disposing of them, put down slug pellets. Slugs feed at night and hide in the day. They are usually only a major problem in warm, wet weather. Basil is far less likely to suffer attack by slugs, or any of these pests, if it is grown on in a pot, rather than planted out in the garden.

Fig 118   Greenfly on roses.

Fig 117   Slugs and snails can be a nuisance in wet weather. If you use slug pellets, put them down at night, when slugs feed, and cover pellets by day to conceal them from birds and pets.

Aphids

This family of plant-lice, which includes greenfly, blackfly and whitefly, are all sap-suckers and capable of causing considerable damage to plants. They flourish in hot dry summers following mild winters. Ladybirds are their natural predators.

If greenfly attack the roses in your herb garden, it may sometimes be necessary to resort to spraying with chemicals, but remember that if you do so you will also harm beneficial insects like ladybirds.

Blackfly sometimes attack the seed heads of angelica, fennel and dill. Cut off and destroy affected parts before the fly can become established. They also like nasturtiums and, notoriously, broad beans. Growing summer savory close by acts as a deterrent. I find the most effective way to deal with them is to hose them off with plain water under pressure, rubbing away where necessary. Alternatively, spray with warm, soapy water. It helps to keep the foliage of plants affected by blackfly well-watered and the area weed-free.

Fig 119   Blackfly on angelica.

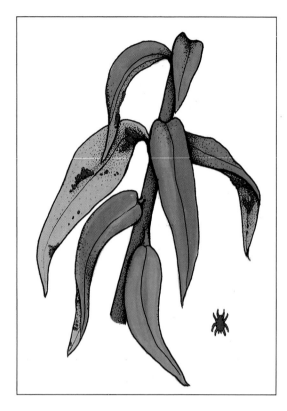

Fig 120   Red spider mite.

Red Spider Mite

This is one of the more persistent pests. It flourishes in hot, dry conditions, such as the greenhouse. Found on the underside of leaves, it is a minute insect which feeds on plant sap. The more succulent-leaved herbs, grown under glass, are vulnerable. Spray plant foliage with a fine rose or mist regularly to ensure a moist atmosphere in the greenhouse, and provide plenty of ventilation.

When buying plants such as lemon verbena, pineapple sage or basil, which have been raised under glass, examine the undersides of leaves carefully to make sure you do not bring in affected plants. If plants become infested later, spraying with liquid derris will usually work.

Cuckoo Spit

This is caused by another sap-sucker, a tiny green or yellow bug, which exudes a mass of white froth to protect itself. Most of the damage is done by the larva of the bug. Since this emerges in late spring, it was erroneously connected with the activities of the cuckoo by country people in the past. Roses, rosemary and southernwood are all sometimes affected. As there are usually not too many on each plant, picking cuckoo spit off by hand is the best way to deal with it.

DISEASES

Damping-Off Disease

This affects seedlings only, basil being especially prone to it. It is caused by a fungus which rots the base and stem of a seedling, making it go black. The young plant then collapses and withers. This disease seems to be more of a problem in a cold, wet season, with plants that are grown under glass. This is probably because it is more difficult to give adequate ventilation when outside temperatures are low.

As with most plant diseases, prevention is better than cure. Pay scrupulous attention to hygiene, making sure you use clean trays and fresh, sterilized compost. Do not sow seedlings too thickly, and thin them out in the tray as soon as they come through. It is also important to ensure that there is good ventilation, and that you do not over-water. Spraying seedlings with Cheshunt compound is recommended by some authorities.

Mint Rust

This is another fungus disease. It can attack all the mints. It starts in the root, and spores gradually spread to stems and leaves, causing them to develop rust-coloured patches and pustules, and wither and drop early in the season. It can occur if plants have been grown in one place for too many years. It is difficult to control it effectively once it has become established. The solution is to dig up and burn all affected plants and start

Fig 121   The only certain way to eradicate mint-rust is to dig up affected plants and burn them.

Fig 122   Powdery mildew on bergamot.

again with fresh stock. Try not to replant in exactly the same spot but, if you have no choice, water the soil first with a disinfectant solution to sterilize it before replanting.

Powdery Mildew

This sometimes affects bergamot and sweet cicely. A greyish mould appears on the leaves. Dusting the leaves with sulphur is a recommended control measure.

PREVENTION OF PESTS AND DISEASES

One of the best ways to avoid trouble is to prevent any build-up of pests or disease. Keep the soil in good heart by adding compost and organic mulches, by weeding and watering and generally tending to its needs. If there are problems, deal with them promptly. Spray aphids away with water before they can get a hold and damage leaves, and root out diseased plants quickly and burn them.

As herbs are usually grown to be picked, as ingredients for food, cosmetics and beauty products, or to make teas and home remedies, it makes sense to keep the use of chemical sprays or toxic substances to a minimum, even if you do not aspire to a totally organic system of gardening. On a small garden scale it is often possible to remove pests by hand, or to wash away by thorough hosing. However, there are times when a little chemical help can prevent disaster, such as spraying the roses and occasionally putting down slug pellets.

Derris dust or derris liquid is recommended for many of the above problems. These are organic products (made from the root of a tropical plant) which will destroy aphids and caterpillars. Unfortunately, derris also destroys beneficial insects – ladybirds, bees and butterflies – so use with care and as rarely as possible. Although purportedly harmless to humans, derris is to some extent toxic. To be on the safe side, do not harvest herbs for two weeks following an application and wash them thoroughly before use.

123

Appendices

I MAKING YOUR OWN COMPOST

If you feel you would like to mix your own compost, here are the basic recipes. Remember, a bushel is a dry measure of 8 gallons (36 litres) or four 2 gallon (9 litre) bucketfuls.

Basic ingredients of Potting Compost

7 parts sterilized loam
3 parts peat
2 parts sharp sand

John Innes Potting Compost No. 1

To each bushel of basic ingredients add:

¾oz (21g) ground limestone or chalk
4 oz (113 g) John Innes base fertilizer

John Innes Potting Compost No. 2

To each bushel of basic ingredients add:

1½oz (42g) ground limestone or chalk
8 oz (227g) John Innes base fertilizer

John Innes Potting Compost No. 3

To each bushel of basic ingredients add:

2¼oz (63g) ground limestone or chalk
12 oz (336g) John Innes base fertilizer

John Innes Seed Compost

2 parts sterilized loam
1 part peat
1 part sharp sand

To each bushel add:

1½oz (42g) superphosphate
¾oz (21g) ground limestone or chalk

John Innes base fertilizer is available ready-made from most horticultural retailers or it can be made from the following recipe:

2 parts hoof and horn
2 parts superphosphate
1 part sulphate of potash

John Innes is not a brand name but a formula used by many different companies.

II HERB NURSERIES

United Kingdom

Opening hours vary considerably, some being very limited. Those marked with an asterisk are known to be open daily during the summer months, but it would be advisable to telephone before visiting to check exact times.

Bradley Gardens Nursery (display garden, mail order)
Sled Lane
Wylam
Northumberland NE41 8JL
Tel: 0661 852176

Brin School Fields
The Old School
Flichity
Inverness IV1 2XD
Tel: 080 83 288

Cheshire Herbs* (courses, talks)
Fourfields
Forest Road
Little Budworth
Nr. Tarporley
Cheshire CW6 9ES
Tel: 0829 760578

The Herb Farm* (closed Mondays, display
garden, barn shop)
Peppard Road,
Sonning Common,
Reading, Berkshire RG4 9NJ
Tel: 0734 724220

The Herb Garden* (display garden)
Hall View Cottage
Hardstoft
Pilsley
Chesterfield
Derbyshire S45 8AH
Tel: 0246 854268

Hill Farm Herbs* (display garden, herb shop,
dried flowers)
Park Walk
Brigstock
Northamptonshire NN14 3HH
Tel: 0536 373694

Hollington Nurseries* (display gardens,
garden design specialist)
Woolton Hill
Newbury
Berkshire RG15 9XT
Tel: 0635 253908

Humber Herbs (display garden, garden design)
The Botanic Gardens
57 Thwaite Street
Cottingham
N. Humberside HU16 4QX
Tel: 0482 875776

Iden Croft Herbs* (display garden, facilities for
people with disabilities)
Frittenden Road
Staplehurst
Kent TN12 0DH
Tel: 0580 891432

Mordon Herbs (display garden)
Mill Farm
Aquhythie
Kemnay
Inverurie
Aberdeenshire AB5 9NY
Tel: 0467 43167

Norfolk Herbs (display garden, garden design)
Mill Farm
Wendling
Dereham
Norfolk NR19 2LY
Tel: 036287 211

Scotherbs* (display garden,
herb cookery courses)
Watery Butts
Grange by Errol
Perthshire PH2 7SZ
Tel: 082 12 228

Selsley Herb Farm* (display garden)
Waterlane
Selsley
Stroud
Gloucestershire TL5 5LW
Tel: 0453 766682

Southwick Country Herbs
(display garden, mail order)
Southwick Farm
Nomansland
Nr. Tiverton
Devon EX16 8NW
Tel: 0884 861099

Suffolk Herbs (herb seed specialists – send for
free catalogue)
Sawyers Farm
Little Cornard
Sudbury
Suffolk CO10 0NY
Tel: 0787 227247

Vivienne Trusler Herb Gardens
(ready-planted herb containers)
42 St Martins
Marlborough
Wiltshire SN8 1AS
Tel: 0672 514244

Waltham Herbs (mail order)
The Herb Shop
Brigsley Road
Waltham
Nr. Grimsby
South Humberside DN36 4QN
Tel: 0472 814129

III GARDENS TO VISIT

Hatfield House
Hatfield
Hertfordshire
Tel: 07072 62823
West Gardens open daily, except Good Friday,
11.00am–6.00pm, March–October.
Festival of Gardening held at midsummer.

Barnsley House
Nr. Cirencester
Gloucestershire
Tel: 028574 281
Open Monday to Saturday 10am–6pm
throughout the year.

Moseley Old Hall
Mosely Old Hall Lane
Wolverhampton
Tel: 0902 782808
Open Saturday and Sunday 2–6pm,
March–October.
Wednesday–Sunday 2–6pm, July–mid-
September.

IV ASSOCIATIONS AND SOCIETIES

United Kingdom

The British Herb Trade Association
Agriculture House
Knightsbridge
London SW1X 7NJ
Tel: 071 235 5077
Fax: 071 235 3526

The Herb Society
PO Box 559
London SW11 4RW
Tel: 0296 625126

United States of America

The International Herb Growers and Marketers
Association
PO Box 281
Silver Spring PA 157575
USA
Tel: 717 285 4252

Australia

The Herb Society of South Australia
PO Box 140
Parkside
S. Australia 5063

New Zealand

The Auckland Herb Society
PO Box 20022
Glen Eden
Auckland 7
New Zealand

Index

(Note: page numbers referring to illustrations appear in italic.)